This Book is dedicated to my beautiful wife, Tameka Pettigrew, and our amazing Young Prince, Austin Pettigrew.

Thank you both for serving as the primary sources of inspiration and support for me during my entire Bridge Building journey.

I Love You!

We Can All Be Bridge Builders; A Leadership Guide to Building Bridges of Trust, Empathy & Understanding for any Organization, Team, or Community

By: Tru Pettigrew

Purpose of this Book: This book exists to serve as a guide to help corporate and community leaders better understand how to Build Bridges across differences and division of all kinds among their teams and community members.

Introduction:
In today's diverse & interconnected world, effective leadership goes far beyond just managing teams and communities. It requires Inclusive Leadership! Being an effective leader requires both the ability, and the willingness, to build bridges of empathy & understanding; fostering an environment where individuals feel valued, heard, and supported.

"Building Bridges," offers readers a comprehensive guide for corporate and community leaders, equipping them with the tools and strategies to help build bridges across areas of division that challenge them most.

Drawing on real-world examples, and expert insights, this thought-provoking book delves into the core principles of leading with empathy and understanding; unveiling the transformative power that leaders seek.

Through the practical advice and action steps provided throughout this book, leaders will learn how to embrace diversity, empathize with the experiences of other people, and create an inclusive culture that celebrates differences.

"Building Bridges" serves as a compass for leaders navigating the complex terrain of modern day leadership. From trust to resolving the most challenging conflicts, this book explores various aspects of leadership through an empathetic lens, offering strategies to navigate these challenges and help enhance communication, all delivered in a very succinct and deliberate way. As leaders embark on this journey of self-discovery and growth, they will be empowered to foster stronger and more meaningful connections, cultivate mutual respect, and inspire their teams and communities to reach their full potential.

Whether you are an established leader in your organization, or an aspiring leader looking to make a difference in the world, this book is an invaluable resource for unlocking the true potential of leadership, and creating lasting positive change.

Contents:

1. My Bridge Building Journey

2. Overview and Expectations of a Bridge Builder

3. The Importance of Empathy and Understanding in Leadership
   a. Creating a Culture of Trust
   b. Defining and Embracing Diversity, Equity & Inclusion
   c. Conflict Resolution
   d. Values-Driven Leadership
   e. Chapter Summary

4. Understanding the Landscape of Differences
   a. Landscape Overview
   b. The Complexity of Difference
   c. Recognition and Respect
   d. Listening and Learning
   e. Empathy and Action
   f. Chapter Summary

5. Cultivating Empathy in Leadership
   a. Defining Leadership & Empathy
   b. Embracing Empathy as a Core Leadership Competency
   c. Empathetic Leadership Tools
   d. Monitoring & Measuring Empathy
   e. Chapter Summary

6. Overcoming Barriers to Reaching an Understanding
   a. Causes and Challenges
   b. Encourage Active Listening
   c. Foster a Culture of Openness
   d. Education and Training
   e. Mindful Communication
   f. Encourage Perspective Taking
   g. Leverage Technology
   h. Challenge Stereotypes
   i. Chapter Summary

7. Building Bridges of Understanding
   a. Understanding the Importance of Inclusivity
   b. Implementing Inclusive Decision-Making
   c. The Way Forward
   d. Chapter Summary

8. Empowering Leaders as Change Agents
      a. Getting Started
      b. Cultivating Self-Awareness
      c. Enhancing Cultural Competence
      d. Facilitating Dialogue
      e. Building Partnerships
      f. Empowering Others
      g. Chapter Summary

9. My Unforgettable 2020 Bridge Building Experience in Minneapolis

10. Lessons, Take-Aways, and Call-to-Action

Chapter 1: My Bridge Building Journey

Hello, my name is Tru Pettigrew, and I am a Bridge Builder. I don't build physical bridges though. I build the types of bridges that help members of society to connect across differences. Those differences include racial divides, gender divides, political divides, generational divides, or relational divides of any kind. And based on my experiences, I am convinced that We Can All Be Bridge Builders!

According to an article published by the United States Studies Centre in March of 2022 (*1), America is the most divided it has ever been since the Civil War. So, it is my contention that we need Bridge Builders now more than ever.

My personal bridge building journey started on Wednesday, August 13,

2014. Some of you may remember, that the previous Saturday, August 9, 2014, that was the day that a white police officer named Darren Wilson shot and killed a young black man named Mike Brown in Ferguson, Missouri (*2). You may also remember all of the racial and social unrest that followed.

That incident sparked national outrage. It also generated a lot of fear, distrust, and animosity towards Law Enforcement. This was particularly true with members of the Black community. And I was no different.

Allow me, however, to provide you with some additional background and context that influenced my thoughts and my feelings towards police at that time.

I'm originally from Baltimore, MD. And the neighborhood where I grew up in Baltimore, was plagued with lots of crime and violence. And the police officers that policed our neighborhood, did so in a very heavy-handed way. So much so, that I found myself on the receiving end of excessive force by the police on numerous occasions. But not just me... it was happening to me and a lot of my friends. To the point where we just normalized it. I also had a few negative experiences with police later in life, beyond my time growing up in Baltimore.

One particular incident that I'll never forget happened when I was living in Los Angeles. I was coming out of a 7-11 one day, and as I was leaving the store, two police cars were pulling into the parking lot, fast and furious! With lights flashing and sirens blaring! The cars came to a screeching halt, officers jumped out with guns drawn, yelling, and screaming. At this point, I was just trying to get out of the way, because clearly something bad was taking place. Next thing I know, one of those officers grabs me, throws me to the ground, with my face pressed against the blacktop of the parking lot, he plants his knee in my back, points his gun right against the side of my head, and yells… "Give me a reason, I wish you would!"

I was confused. And I was afraid. I had no idea what was going on or why. I was arrested that day.

Fortunately for me, that incident never led to any jail time, because while I was being detained, some other officers caught the right guy at a completely different 7-11. As it was explained to me, the officers that grabbed me were responding to a call of a 7-11 being robbed at gunpoint, and somehow showed up at the wrong store location. They went on to explain to me that I fit the description of the suspect, and the whole situation was just a case of mistaken identity.

That incident, coupled with several of my other experiences growing up in Baltimore, all led to me not liking, or trusting police.

So yeah, when Mike Brown was shot and killed in Ferguson, MO, it affected me in a way that I didn't quite understand at the time. But I have a much better understanding now.

You see… my wife and I have a 12-year-old son (at the time of the writing of this book); My Young Prince. His name is Austin. Austin was only 2 years old when the incident in Ferguson occurred, and me and my family were living in Cary, NC. And for those of you who may not be familiar with Cary, it's important to know that Cary is a predominantly white, and also a relatively affluent community. And with the seemingly non-stop reports of unarmed Black Men being shot and killed by police all across the country during that time, I was concerned for my son's safety.

Because my thoughts about a town like Cary, were that the police were there to protect and serve its white citizens and community members, but to police its Black citizens and community members. The burning questions for me then became... how do I protect my son from all the things that I'm seeing in the news? How do I protect him from the very things that happened to me? How do I protect my young son from white police officers that may see him as a threat, simply because of the color of his skin?

I had no answers. I felt a sense of helplessness and hopelessness. I don't wish that feeling on anyone. Especially a father when it comes to protecting his children. And it was in that moment, that I gained a deeper understanding of a Father's Love! You see... it was my Love for my son that compelled me to face my fears head on. And on Wednesday, August 13, 2014, just four days after Mike Brown was shot and killed in Ferguson, I walked through the doors of Cary's Police Department. I walked through those doors with the hopes of building a relationship that could potentially save my son's life.

The day that I walked through those doors, I met with an officer named Jeremy Burgin (my man JB), who eventually introduced me to the Deputy Police Chief at the time, Tony Godwin. In my initial meeting with the Deputy Chief, I remember expressing my fears, frustrations, and concerns for my son's safety. I even shared my own experiences that led to those concerns.

The response that I received was not what I expected. These are the words that Chief Godwin shared with me almost verbatim…

"Tru, I'm sorry that those things happened to you. And I'm sorry that you have to carry so much angst regarding the safety of your son. How can I help? How can I change the way you feel about the Cary PD and this profession that I love?"

I wasn't ready for that response. I was expecting him to be dismissive, defensive, and even accusatory to some degree. But instead, he was empathetic, compassionate, and understanding.

He then went on to challenge me. He asked me if I could help him, and his officers, change the hearts and minds of other members in the Black community, that may feel and think the same way as I did. And I accepted that challenge.

My response to the challenge, was an invitation for Chief Godwin and his officers to join me at a local Black-Owned Barbershop in Cary, to engage in some difficult, but also very critical conversations with the Black Community. The name of the barbershop was Headliners. He agreed, and we started a series called Barbershop Rap Sessions.

These discussions were facilitated dialogues between the Police and the Black Community. During these discussions, we all exchanged our diverse perspectives and various lived experiences with each other. The outcome was a collection of beautifully co-created thoughts, ideas, and solutions, on how we could build the most welcoming, most inclusive, and most equitable community possible, for us all to thrive.

Those Barbershop Rap Sessions began in September of 2014 and continued up until March of 2023. We met consistently on the first Saturday of every month for 9 years straight! We even continued our meetings during the pandemic by going virtual.

And when the tragic murder of George Floyd occurred in the city of Minneapolis in May of 2020 (*3), an executive that was working for the Minnesota Timberwolves NBA team was familiar with the Bridge Building work that I was doing. He reached out to me and asked if I would lead some discussions with the team, to help them navigate their feelings around everything that was taking place. I accepted. And after several successful Bridge Building Sessions with the team, I was extended an offer to serve as the organizations first ever Chief Diversity, Equity, and Inclusion Officer. I began serving in that role in 2020, and in 2022, the role evolved to me serving as Chief Impact Officer. I served in that role up until 2024, and during my time in Minneapolis, I invested quite a bit of my time, talent, and treasure as a Community Bridge Builder throug out the city. The whole time, I was gaining a much greater awareness and appreciation for the value and impact of empathy & understanding when it comes to Building Bridges across differences.

Serving as Chief Impact Officer for the Minnesota Timberwolves & Lynx, as well as investing my time as a Community Bridge Builder in a city with such an amazing group of DEI Champions taught me a lot. I am truly grateful for the Minnesota Timberwolves & Lynx CEO, Ethan Casson for his Inclusive Leadership style, and the many lessons I was able to glean from him along the way. I also have to give a major shout out to Timberwolves Head of Security, Tony Adams, for all the valuable lessons I learned from him.

I am also fortunate and extremely grateful for the opportunity to have learned from, and to have been able to Build Bridges of empathy and understanding alongside, some of the absolute best DEI Leaders in the nation. That list includes names like Greg Cunningham of US Bank, James Burroughs of Childrens MN, Amelia Hardy of Best Buy, Kiera Fernandez of Target, Tracey Gibson of Andersen Corporation, Rod Young and Kathie Eiland-Madison of Delta Dental Minnesota, and several others. Thank you all!

When I started my Bridge Building journey it was personal. The journey was fueled by my love for my son. As I've stated above, I've learned some valuable lessons along the way. I've also had my fair share of surprises. And one of my biggest surprises, is the bond that I've built with Chief Tony Godwin, the former Police Chief of Cary, NC. Or as I like to call him, my brother TG. He has become one of the closest people to me on this planet.

And if you would have told me, a year before TG and I met, that one of my closest friends in the world would be a white male Police Chief from the South, I would have never believed you.

So, I am convinced, that if someone like me, who at one point in my life did not like, and did not trust, any police officers... if I can build bridges of trust, empathy, and love like I've done with my brother TG, and so many other officers around the world since then, I believe We Can All Be Bridge Builders!

Before I go any further, here are two Bridge Building Principles that I want to challenge you all to start applying in your lives today!

The first is *Make Time to Engage!* I know that we're all busy. And I also know that making time to engage with people that are different from you, can be inconvenient, and even uncomfortable at times. But please understand this… the temporary sting of inconvenience and any level of discomfort you may feel from making the time to engage, pales in comparison to all of the long-term consequences of division you will experience from not making the time.

The second, is this… *Manage Your Information Sources!* What I mean by that, is don't allow your primary information source about people that don't look like you, to only come from people that look like you. In other words, if you are a white person, and all the information that you've ever studied, learned, or even believed about black people, came from other white people, then I'd encourage you to check the source. The same is true if you are black when it comes to your thoughts about white people, or any other race or ethnicity.

I'm often asked, Tru… what type of person truly has what it takes to be a Bridge Builder. My answer always remains the same… all of us.
We Can All Be Bridge Builders! It is my hope, that the information in this book will help you to start building those bridges, and to keep building those bridges in any and all areas of difference and division in your life.

Chapter 2: Overview and Expectations of a Bridge Builder

Considering that every single family, community, city, state, and country, are all filled with so many diverse perspectives, experiences, and backgrounds; one would think that connecting across differences would be a natural and harmonious process. Yet, as you look around, it becomes painfully clear that hurt, pain, and destruction are all too common outcomes of our collective inability to build bridges across the gaps that divide us.

In the corporate landscape, where collaboration and cooperation are essential for success, this inability to build bridges across differences takes a toll in areas of productivity, employee morale, and ultimately, the bottom line. But these issues extend far beyond boardroom walls, permeating our communities and undermining the very fabric of our society. It is time to confront this pressing issue head-on and explore the transformative power of bridge building.

In this book, we will dive deep into the heart of the matter, examining the roots of the problem while also offering actionable strategies to help foster authentic and meaningful connections across differences. Get ready to embark on a journey of self-discovery, empathy, and growth, as you uncover the impact that building bridges can have on corporate environments and diverse communities alike. Together, let us embark on a mission to heal, unite, and create a world where our unique differences are celebrated and our collective potential truly knows no bounds.

Chapter 3: The Importance of Empathy and Understanding in Leadership

Creating a Culture of Trust

Empathetic leaders recognize that their success is intrinsically tied to the success and well-being of their teams. By establishing a culture of trust and engagement, leaders can create an environment where each individual feels valued, supported, and empowered. Through applying basic principles like active listening, compassionate communication, and a genuine interest in employees' experiences, leaders can build greater rapport and forge stronger connections. This can help lead to increased employee loyalty, higher levels of motivation, and improved productivity, as individuals begin to feel understood and appreciated for their unique contributions.

Defining and Embracing Diversity, Equity & Inclusion

Diversity, by definition, is the state of being different. It is not relegated to categories of race, age, gender, or sexual orientation. Something that I believe is worth pointing out about the definition of diversity, is it is a "state of being". Diversity, on its own, does not do anything. It is, however, an amazing gift. And it is a gift that is available to us all. But in order to benefit from that gift, you must first recognize and appreciate the gift, and then be willing to go *beyond diversity*, to actively engage in equity, and inclusion. We'll talk more about the impact of equity and the power of inclusion shortly. As for now, there are 3 more things you should know about the definition of diversity, and those are the three primary forms of diversity.

The three primary forms of diversity are Identity Diversity, Experiential Diversity, and Cognitive Diversity.

Identity Diversity is what you see when you look at someone. You see what you perceive to be someone's identity based on the color of their skin, their perceived gender based on how you've been conditioned to associate gender, and even their age based on how young or old they may appear to you. In other words, you can look at someone and automatically assume or believe they are a Gen Z White Female, or a Baby Boomer Black Male.

Experiential Diversity is based on your individual lived experiences. And we all have very unique lived experiences that differ from others; especially those with different racial, ethnic, gender, and generational identities than us. Your experiential diversity is not only influenced by your identity, but it's also influenced by other factors, like geography, economics, education, and even parenting styles.

Cognitive Diversity is all about how differently you think and how you process information. Also, how you approach problem solving and the way you engage and interact with others. We all have very different approaches to problem solving, conflict resolution, and ideation, when it comes to the development of new and innovative products, services, and solutions.

Cognitive Diversity is arguably the most valuable form of diversity among the three. Because it is through diversity of thought, that you are able to generate new and innovative ideas and solutions that go beyond what already exists. This is not to suggest that the other forms of diversity are not valuable, because they are. As much as some people would like to treat them all independently of one another, you can't separate the connections that exist between any of these 3 forms of diversity. You see... your identity diversity influences your experiential diversity, which then informs your cognitive diversity. In other words, because I identify as a Generation X, cisgender, Black Male; my lived experiences (experiential diversity) have differed significantly from that of a Queer, Millennial, White Female. And not because either of us chose the experiences that we've had, but mostly because we both have been required to navigate life differently because of how society views us and treats us. And it is our unique lived experiences, that informs our Cognitive Diversity. So, although these 3 different forms of diversity are all distinct, they are all still very strongly linked.

That wraps up the definition and discussion on Diversity. Now let's discuss the definition of Equity.

The definition of Equity according to dictionary.com, is fair and impartial treatment. In any corporate or community setting, this can also be defined as meeting people where they are, or ensuring that you are giving people what they need to succeed. Keeping in mind, that people are all at different points on their respective journey's, and that everyone doesn't need the same thing. And we often believe that if we do not treat everyone the exact same way, then we are not being fair. This is how equity can often get confused with equality. Equality is treating everyone the same, while equity is ensuring that you give each individual what they need to succeed.

An example of equity at work could be providing accessible ramps for any team members or community members that are in wheelchairs. Equality, would be expecting them to take the steps like everyone else.

Now, let's define inclusion.

Inclusion by definition is the act of making sure someone feels a sense of belonging. The operative word in this definition is "feel". Because it absolutely does matter how our words and actions make people feel. We have gotten to a point in corporate settings where we believe people's feelings don't matter. We somehow believe that a person's feelings should not be prioritized, and that we should focus strictly on data, facts, and analytics to assess and evaluate business imperatives and objectives. And as important as the numbers, data, and analytics are, it's also important to note that behavioral performance is based much more on a person's emotion than their intellect.

The part of the brain that processes information and data serves as a repository for information. Basically, it functions as a data storage bank, and that's its only function. The part of the brain that compels us to take action, or behave a certain way, is the part of the brain that controls emotion. So, if we want to increase levels of people engagement, and improve overall performance and productivity, it does matter how we make people feel, and that we are intentional about ensuring that they "feel" a strong sense of belonging.

Empathy and understanding are both vital tools for navigating the complexities of diversity, equity, and inclusion within organizations. Leaders who possess an in-depth understanding of their employees' diverse backgrounds, experiences, and perspectives, are much better equipped to create a more inclusive environment, where everyone feels a sense of belonging, welcomed, and respected. By empathizing with the various challenges faced by marginalized groups, leaders can champion equitable policies, help address biases, and help ensure that underrepresented voices are heard and valued. This fosters a greater sense of belonging, further improves creativity, and helps drive innovation within the organization.

Conflict Resolution
Conflict is an inevitable part of any leadership role. However, inclusive and empathetic leaders approach conflict resolution with compassion, seeking to explore and understand the underlying causes and potential motivations behind the discord. By being active listeners, practicing empathy, and facilitating open and honest dialogue, leaders can foster a collaborative environment where conflicts among team members are addressed constructively. And agreeable resolutions are reached

with the interests of all parties in mind. This is an approach that not only minimizes friction, but it also cultivates a culture of trust and teamwork, allowing the organization to overcome challenges and thrive.

Here are what I refer to as the 5 C's of Inclusive Leadership.

1. Confidence
2. Competence
3. Commitment
4. Consistency
5. Care

You may have seen or maybe even have worked with many leaders who display the first 4 C's of Confidence, Competence, Commitment, and Consistency. But it's that 5th C of Care, that will catapult you from a positional leader to an Inclusive Leader. It's when you embrace the 5th C of Care, that you will enhance your ability to become a champion of conflict resolution. When you genuinely care about the well-being of all of your community or team members and how your actions and decisions contribute to the greater good of all, that is the mark of an Inclusive Leader. And it is the "care" attribute that will better equip you in the art of conflict resolution and achieving greater collaboration across differences.

I refer to these attributes as the 5 C's of Inclusive Leadership based on the 4 C's model of evaluating the quality of a diamond. If you've ever purchased a diamond, then you may recall the evaluation criteria of a diamond is categorized as the 4 C's of Color, Clarity, Carat, and Cut. In my experience with purchasing diamonds, there is a very evident 5th C that is not immediately shared or discussed in the evaluation process. And that is Cost! This is how I decided to go with the 5 C's of Inclusive Leadership; because I view Inclusive Leadership to be as rare as a diamond. It also requires us to dig deep, withstand a lot of pressure, and go through a refining process in order for us to achieve the desired result.

Here is a helpful 3-step Conflict Resolution process that you can employ to help you become a stronger Inclusive Leader when you find yourself addressing conflict in your organization or community...

1. Awareness - It is important that you are aware that there is conflict. Because without awareness, there is no need or desire to effect change. The awareness step of the process requires that you have an understanding of the situation with a willingness to openly reflect on how the conflict may have emerged.

2. Acceptance - You must accept that there is a conflict. Additionally, you must accept the circumstance, environment, and even emotional state that the conflict has created; for you and others. Being in denial about the conflict will prohibit you from proceeding to the next step of the process, which is taking action.

3. Action - Once you've become aware, and accepted that a conflict exists, you must then be willing to take the necessary and appropriate action to address and resolve it. And the action must be inclusive of those with whom the conflict exists. Even if it feels uncomfortable. If the actions are not inclusive, the other party or parties involved will not be committed to achieving resolution. Remember, where there is little to no inclusion, there is little to no commitment.

Values-Driven Leadership
Empathy and understanding often serve as guiding forces for inspiring ethical decision-making and value

driven leadership. By considering the impact of your actions on the various stakeholders, you're better equipped to make more informed decisions that align with the overall organizational values and purpose. You are also more likely to prioritize what's best for the greater good over personal gain, and exhibit transparency and integrity in your interactions. Such leaders inspire trust, build credibility, and create a positive reputation for the company, organization, or community. This is the type of leadership that attracts top talent, loyal customers, and valuable strategic partnerships.

Chapter Summary

Empathy and understanding are not merely abstract concepts but they are practical tools that can help transform leadership practices and drive positive change in corporate and community settings alike. By cultivating these qualities, you are better equipped to build bridges across diverse perspectives. It also places you in a better position to promote collaboration, and nurture inclusive environments where all people can thrive. The journey to becoming a more empathetic and understanding leader begins with self-reflection and a commitment to continuous growth. As we embark on this path, we set the stage for a future where empathy and understanding serve as the cornerstones of effective leadership, shaping a better world for us all.

Chapter 4: Understanding the Landscape of Differences

Landscape Overview
In the quest to build empathy and understanding, one of your most crucial and often most challenging tasks will be mapping out the landscape of differences within a group or community. Whether you are working at or navigating the landscape of a multinational corporation with employees from around the globe, or a local community group composed of various racial, ethnic, religious, or political backgrounds; it is imperative to recognize, embrace, and celebrate these differences in order to build bridges of empathy and understanding.

The world that we live in today is the most diverse it has ever been, and growing more and more diverse everyday. These degrees of diversity span across race, ethnicity, gender, age, generation, abilities, and so many more areas. In America alone, there are five different generations in the workplace right now (*4), women-owned businesses are the fastest growing business segment (*5), the LGBTQAI+ community is estimated to have a population of somewhere between 15-17 million people in America (*6), People with disabilities represent well over 61 million Americans (*7), Hispanics are the largest ethnic minority (*8), Blacks are the largest racial minority (*9), Asians are listed as the fastest growing ethnic minority (*10), and minority purchasing power has been reported as exceeding $3.9 trillion dollars (*11).

Something important to keep in mind as it relates to the landscape of difference, is that it is through our differences that we are able to learn, grow, and evolve. We do this through the sharing and exchange of more innovative and creative thoughts, ideas, and solutions, all based on our diversity.

The Complexity of Difference

Differences in a group aren't limited to surface-level demographics like race, religion, or nationality. They span a vast and complex terrain, encompassing our personal beliefs, values, experiences, and ideas. People's backgrounds and identities shape the lens through which they view and interact with the world. These perspectives and lenses are as varied as the people themselves. Leaders need to recognize, respect, and navigate these complexities in order to foster a culture of inclusion.

Recognition and Respect

The first steps towards gaining a deeper understanding the landscape of differences is recognition and respect. This is something that you must proactively pursue. This requires you to proactively seek-out information about all the unique identities, experiences, and varied perspectives that exist within your organization or community. And then respect those differences. This could be done through diversity training programs, surveys, one-on-one conversations, courageous community conversations, and a host of other means. The goal isn't just to collect information, but seek to actively acknowledge the diverse identities and experiences within your group. Once you've identified and acknowledged the diversity within your group, the next step is to make them a recognized part of your collective identity. And a part of respecting those differences is to not be dismissive of other people's realities, experiences, and beliefs, just because they are not your own.

Listening and Learning

Another critical step to building, maintaining, and growing a healthy culture of empathy & understanding, is listening and learning. You should be actively seeking to understand the unique perspectives and lived experiences of individuals within your group. One way you can do this is through conducting listening sessions. This goes beyond passive listening, and truly embracing the art of active listening. This is done by asking open-ended questions, and providing safe spaces for your people to express their views and experiences without fear of any judgement or backlash. The process of listening, learning, and growing is ongoing—it doesn't stop once you've heard from everyone, but needs to be continually practiced and ingrained in the culture of your organization or community. As the saying goes… listen to understand, not just to reply.

Empathy and Action
Finally, understanding the landscape of differences must lead to action. Empathy involves putting oneself in another's shoes, trying to understand their perspective and feelings. This can be challenging, especially when you're dealing with perspectives vastly different from your own, but it's a vital component of building bridges of empathy. Please note, however, that empathy alone is not enough—it must be coupled with action. These actions could be as simple as implementing policies and practices that respect and celebrates differences, that helps to address inequities, and creates an environment where everyone feels seen and heard.

Building empathy must start with story-telling; where there is an openness to information sharing, and to active listening, and learning. But it cannot stop there. Once the story-telling, the listening, and the learning have taken place, then as modern day philosopher Reginald Noble boldly stated… "it's time for some action!"

Chapter Summary
Although understanding the landscape of differences can be a very complex process, it can also be very rewarding. It requires a high level of self awareness, and the awareness of others. It also requires acknowledgement of others, active listening, perpetual learning, leading with empathy, and deliberate action. By making the time to embrace these principles, you can effectively build those bridges of empathy and understanding. And my experience has taught me that theses are the leadership behaviors that lead to a culture that embraces diversity, promotes equity, fosters inclusion, and ultimately drives the collective success of the group.

A proven and effective tool that you can use when you are seeking to better understand the landscape of difference is this 4-Step MEET Model. This model is based on the principle of meeting people where they are. The 4-Step MEET Model breaks down as follows…

M - Make time to engage
E - Explore similarities & differences
E - Encourage respect
T - Take responsibility

Chapter 5: Cultivating Empathy in Leadership

Defining Leadership & Empathy

Leadership is not a position or title; it's action and example. This mantra is widely recognized, but a crucial aspect that is often overlooked, is the indispensable role of empathy in effective leadership.

Here is my personal definition of leadership that I would like to offer you…

Leadership is the process of influencing people, by providing them with purpose, vision, and direction, to accomplish the greater good of the organization or team.

Upon further review of the above definition, you will notice four P words that stand out, and will serve as the core principles I will be using to define and discuss leadership.

Those four P words are *process*, *people*, *providing*, and *purpose*. Each of the words are unpacked in more detail below, to emphasize its role and significance as it relates to defining leadership.

Process - Let us first understand that leadership is a process. It's what you do. It's how you show up. And the behavior that you display when you show up. Leadership is a verb, not a noun. It is an action word. Leadership should be defined by your actions much more than your status or title.

People - Leadership should always be about the people. Leadership should always be viewed as a role of responsibility that you have to the people to whom you've been given stewardship, versus a position of authority that you lord over people. Too often, many of the people that have received leadership positions based on title alone, prioritize things like the bottom line or profit margins *over* the people. Unfortunately, this approach completely negates the understanding that it is the people who help you to achieve those benchmarks and goals.

Providing - A primary focus of every great and inclusive leader should be, if and how, you provide your people with the resources they need to succeed. And the questions you should be asking yourself are; what are you doing to ensure the personal and professional growth and development of your people? And are you providing them with the tools and resources necessary to reach their full potential? And if you are not providing your people with the resources and tools that they need to succeed, then the next question should be why not?

Purpose - This should be at the foundation of every inclusive leader. As Myles Munroe once said; "when you don't know the purpose of something, abuse is inevitable". Knowing the reason you are doing something, and providing that same clarity of purpose to others, is paramount to inclusive leadership.

Clarity of purpose provides what I call a VIP experience for the leaders and everyone else around them. But unlike the standard acronym for VIP of Very Important People (which still applies), this VIP stands for Value, Impact, and Precision. When you have clarity of purpose and are able to provide that for others, it gives people more *Value* to where they are going, more *Impact* to what they are doing, and more *Precision* to how they do it. In short, having clarity of purpose provides a VIP Experience for you and everyone else around you… Value, Impact, and Precision!

Empathy, defined as the ability to understand and share the feelings of others, is the cornerstone that bridges the gap between corporate objectives and community welfare. It underpins a leader's capacity to form deep connections with all stakeholders, inspiring trust, deeper commitment, and mutual understanding. Please note, this chapter is designed specifically to present practical strategies for cultivating empathy in leadership, that helps to foster environments where your corporate success aligns with the betterment of society.

I believe empathy & understanding are best developed through storytelling. It is very difficult for us to develop a healthy level of empathy for someone if we don't know their story. To best exercise our empathy muscles, I think it's important that we understand how someone feels about a particular topic or subject and more importantly, why they feel they way they do.

And similar to diversity, there are three primary forms of empathy. Those three-forms are Cognitive Empathy, Emotional Empathy, and Compassionate Empathy. Each form is further explained below. And keep in mind… empathy is about understanding, not agreement.

1. Cognitive Empathy - Developing cognitive empathy allows you to understand how someone else *think*s about a situation and why they *think* the way that they do.

2. Emotional Empathy - Emotional empathy allows you to understand how someone else *feels* about a certain situation and why they *feel* they way they do.

3. Compassionate Empathy - Your compassionate empathy is born out of a combination of your combined cognitive and emotional empathy. Once your cognitive and emotional levels of empathy are in place, compassionate empathy is a feeling you possess that compels you to leverage your own power, position, platform, and privilege to help change the circumstances that may be causing someone else feelings of exclusion, marginalization, or any form of oppression.

Embracing Empathy as a Core Leadership Competency

Empathy is more than a soft skill; it's a strategic asset. Understanding its value begins with a shift in your mindset. I encourage leaders to perceive empathy not as a liability but as a strength. Those that lead with empathy can effectively gauge the emotional climate of their teams. This leads to an improved level of decision-making, conflict resolution, and overall productivity. Research, including organizational behavior and neuroscience, reinforces the connection between empathy, trust, and organizational performance (*12). It's always helpful to promote a culture where empathy is both celebrated and encouraged from the top down.

Empathetic Leadership Tools:
- **Active Listening:** Empathy begins by genuinely listening to others to understand, and not just listening to respond. Leaders can show they care by giving others their full attention, acknowledging their feelings, and realizing that their perspectives are valid.

- **Open-ended Conversations:** Do your best to promote dialogue that encourages other people to express their thoughts, feelings, and emotions freely. This enables leaders to tap into the emotions, needs, and desires of their team members, resulting in deeper empathy and understanding.

- **Emotional Intelligence:** Regular workshops aimed at enhancing leaders' emotional intelligence can significantly improve their empathetic skills. These sessions should include exercises that help focus on understanding emotions, properly managing those emotions, and interacting with others empathetically.

- **Walking in their Shoes:** Foster situations that require leaders to experience the perspectives of their team members, and other stakeholders and community members. Immersion experiences or role-reversal exercises can help provide you with a much more profound understanding of others' realities.

- **Practice Mindfulness:** Take time to encourage mindfulness, as it helps leaders to be present in their interactions. Exactly what is 'mindfulness' you ask? Great question - *Mindfulness is defined as being aware of one's internal states and surroundings.* When you practice mindfulness, it can help to reduce destructive habits, responses, and behaviors by learning to observe thoughts, emotions, and other experiences that occur in the moment without immediately judging or reacting to them. In other words, take time to live in the present moment. Be intentional about being more aware and more fully engaged with what is happening around you without judgement. Some ways to practice mindfulness can be as simple as slowing down, taking a walk, focus on your breathing, or taking inventory of who and what is around you.

- **Make Time to Engage:** We are all busy. And with the advent and rapid growth of modern day technology, it is becoming even more challenging to slow down and converse with people face to face. Please note, however, that the temporary inconvenience you may feel from making the time to engage with others, pales in comparison to the potential long term consequences that could emerge from not making the time to engage.

- **Feedback Culture:** Constructive feedback helps leaders understand how their actions affect others, and promotes empathetic behavior. Regular 360-degree feedback meetings and sessions can be particularly effective.

Monitoring & Measuring Empathy
Though it is seemingly abstract, empathy can be monitored and measured. Tools such as empathy mapping, some of the different emotional intelligence assessments, and 360-degree feedback sessions, are just a few tools that can help provide valuable insights into a leader's empathetic prowess. These regular assessments enable leaders to understand their growth areas, set empathy-related goals, and track their progress over time.

For me, one of the most fascinating tools for measuring empathy that I have run across is a technique called empathy mapping. It was created by a business strategist named Dave Gray, and has been used primarily to help businesses understand how people think and feel about different products and services (*13). And because of the empathy map's ability to help teams use emotional intelligence to gain insights into the hearts and minds of a specific target audience, I saw and found value in also using it as a tool to benefit individuals and teams when it comes to understanding how people feel about situations, cultures, and environments. And more importantly, why they feel the way that they do.

Keeping in mind that, if you can empathize with others, they will more than likely reciprocate, making it much easier for individuals to connect, cooperate, and collaborate as a team.

Empathy Mapping offers a series of prompts to help identify the thoughts, feelings, drivers, and needs of a specific target audience. This allows the individuals that are participating in the exercise to focus on the needs and requirements of the target audience instead of their own; thus building up your cognitive and emotional empathy in the process.

Below are the steps to conducting Empathy Mapping exercises per David Gray's book *Gamestorming: A Playbook for Innovators, Rule-breakers, and Changemakers.*

Step 1: Establish Focus and Goals
Who is the person or people group that is the focus of the map?
This is the audience you want to understand and empathize with. Do your best to assess and summarize their situation, and their current role within the organization, culture, or community. If you have multiple personas, each one will need their own map.

What is the desired outcome?
This is what you hope will change. What does success look like? For example… is there an attitudinal, behavioral, or emotional difference in how the designated subject or people group of the map shows up,

that indicates that they don't feel a sense of belonging? What role do they play in achieving the change they seek? Keep in mind that this exercise is about building empathy for a greater sense of belonging, and answering the "desired outcome" question will help to create focus for the participants and set context for the activity.

Step 2: Capture their Outside World

Although there is no set order for completing each section of the process, Empathy Mapping creator, Dave Gray, suggests that it is more productive to start with observable activities that are taking place in the world of the audience member(s) being mapped. Participants often generate these more easily than the more introspective steps. Start by examining the daily experience of the person or people group being mapped, and imagine what it's like to be them. Complete the sections of the map to capture what they see, say, do, and hear everyday.

What do they SEE?
What are they encountering in their daily experiences? These could be people, activities, or things. What are the people around them doing? What are they watching, reading, and exposed to within their work environment or community that could influence them? Aspects to consider include co-workers, family, friends, news media, social media, etc. Remember this is their world, not yours, so don't assume that what you're experiencing on a daily basis is the same thing that they are experiencing.

What do they DO and SAY?
What are their behaviors and how do they conduct themselves? What is their attitude and what are the things they are saying to you? Think

about how these things might change depending on where they are, who they are with, or who is nearby. Attitude can be viewed as actions towards others or the tone and manner in which they convey something. If applicable, note how their behavior changes in a public versus private settings. Examples or questions to consider here are things like... do they show up on social media differently than they do in person? How do they use social media? Do they even use social media at all? What work events do they choose to attend or avoid? Do they participate in company potlucks, happy hours, or any other social gatherings?

What do they HEAR?
What are they hearing and how is it influencing them? Consider their personal connections with family, friends, and coworkers along with what is being said in the different

news mediums. What types of news information do they hear from on-air personalities, influencers on social media, podcasters, and experts in various fields. Focus on things that impact their thinking and mental health. Key influencers should focus on the people, places, or things that influence how they act and make decisions.

Step 3: Explore Inside the Mind
After completing all of the outside elements, the focus moves inside the mind to explore the thoughts and feelings that are internal and that are not necessarily observable. These might be inferred, guessed, or captured in direct quotes you may have heard from them. This is the central point of the exercise, as teams imagine what it is like to be in someone else's headspace. This exercise should be conducted with the understanding that it is virtually impossible to know exactly what

someone else is thinking or even how they are feeling. The goal here is to do your best to place yourself in their headspace and heart-space based on your newfound revelation from all of the external drivers and influencers in their lives.

What do they THINK and FEEL?
What matters most to them? What are they thinking about? Consider positive and negative sides of thoughts. What makes them feel good or bad? What do they worry about or what keeps them up at night? What gets them going in the morning? Consider that a persons mind is exploring various paths and possibilities as they consider doing or trying something; especially something new. How do they feel about these new pursuits? Are they Frightened? Excited? Anxious? Confident?

Next, take time to explore the specifics of their pains and gains. What does success and failure look like? Capture potential frustrations, challenges, and any obstacles that may stand in their way. What goals and dreams do they have?

Step 4: Summarize and Share
When all the sections are complete, take a moment to reflect. Have the participants share their thoughts on the experience. Ask how it changed their perspectives or if it produced new insights. Capture conclusions and ideas the team generated, take pictures, or create a new electronic version for sharing online. If you work in an office, consider placing the original empathy map in a public area or creating poster versions to share. These are just a few ways to expose others in the organization to the persona and to help encourage them to lead with empathy.

I also suggest soliciting feedback from the people or people groups that were the focus of your empathy mapping exercise once the exercise is complete. After all, they are the experts on themselves. And as they saying goes… "please don't make decisions about me without me."

Remember, empathy mapping is a tool and not a solution to achieving an entire organizational mind shift. Circulating empathy map photos is not going to translate into a sudden willingness to empathize with others if it isn't something that is a part of the broader company culture. The purpose of the exercise is to place individuals or audiences who are not reflected in the organization's majority population, at the center of the participants' minds. If the process of conducting this exercise leaves a lasting impact on those who participated, then it's done its job, and consider it a success.

See Figure 1 below for an example of an Empathy Map illustration…

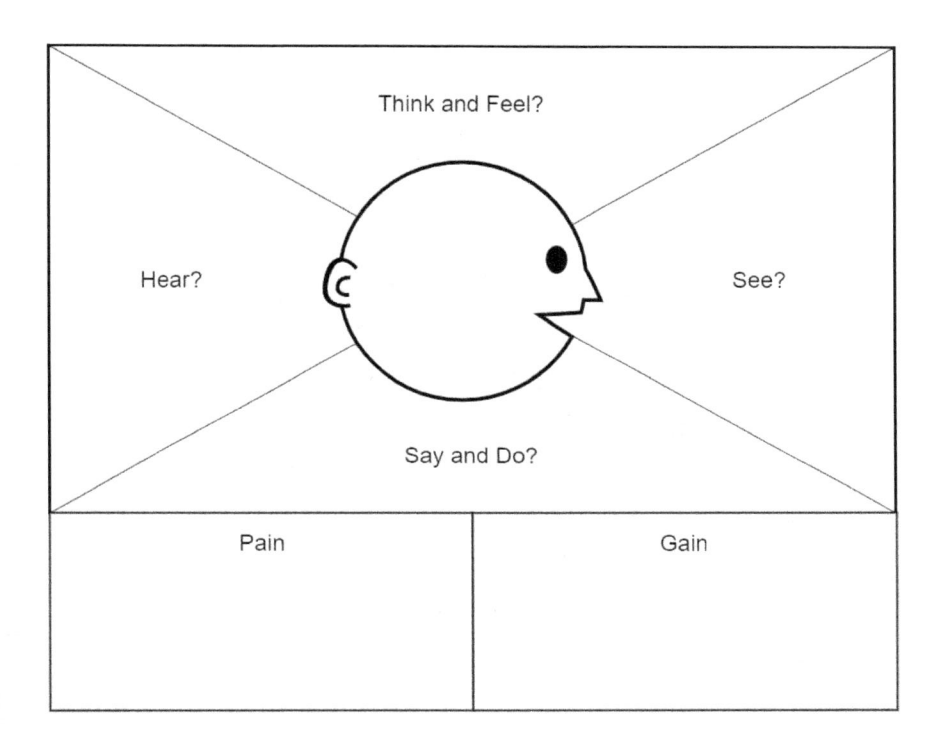

Think and Feel?

Hear?

See?

Say and Do?

Pain

Gain

Figure 1 Source: Empathy Map Canvas by Dave Gray

Chapter Summary
Empathy in leadership is an ongoing journey, not a destination. It requires constant nurturing, practice, and assessment. As you become a more empathetic leader, expect to see a vast improvement in your teams morale, productivity, and overall team engagement, collaboration, and integration. As we look to the future, the future of leadership is empathetic. And by building bridges of empathy and understanding, you can look forward to a culture that thrives on collaboration, our shared humanity, and a strong sense of purpose.

Chapter 6: Overcoming Barriers to Reaching Understanding

Causes and Challenges

Barriers to understanding, often subconscious and deeply rooted in our biases and behaviors, are among the biggest challenges we face when it comes to building bridges with those that we see as different from us. These barriers can spring from our preconceptions, our unconscious biases, geography, culture, language, and a host of other potential sources. For leaders to be able to maximize performance and productivity among their teams, overcoming these barriers is a must. When you can take the steps to overcome these barriers and help others to do the same, the result is an environment of mutual respect, an appreciation for difference, and a sense of belonging for all.

The following section offers some strategies to help navigate these obstacles effectively.

Encourage Active Listening

We've discussed the importance of active listening in the earlier section on listening & learning, and this point cannot be emphasized enough. Oftentimes, the barriers to understanding come from the failure to listen and to listen actively. Active listening entails fully focusing on, understanding, and responding to a speaker, showing genuine interest in what they're saying. As opposed to competitive listening, which is when the listener is listening for ways to debate or discredit whatever the speaker is saying in an effort to prove them wrong, or to prove themselves right. When you employ competitive listening, you simply creates more division, discord and dysfunction.

Foster a Culture of Openness
Another component to overcoming barriers to understanding is creating an environment where individuals feel safe and valued in sharing their perspectives. This will require that you establish norms and policies that encourages the sharing and expressing of diverse thoughts. This will need to permeate from the top so that team members and staff can sense the companies support, and trust that leadership truly does value differing viewpoints. This does not mean that everyone's thoughts and ideas will be implemented. It just means that you believe everyone's voice matters and that you value people's thoughts and ideas. When people feel comfortable being open to sharing their thoughts and ideas in a workplace environment, this can result in greater job satisfaction, higher levels of retention, less stress, and more innovative ideas.

Education and Training

Regular training on empathy, bias, and cultural sensitivity can go a long way in breaking down barriers. These programs can help people recognize and even overcome their biases. It can also help to develop the skills needed to empathize with others, and gain a better understanding of the different cultures, perspectives, and experiences of others. Allocate the time and the budget for employees for growth and professional development, along with specific action steps and success measures for how to go about achieving their goals. Taking the time to create and fund ERGs (Employee Resources Groups) or BRGs (Business Resource Groups), is another great way to contribute to the education, the training, and the professional development of your teams.

An ERG or BRG is an employee-led initiative that exists to foster a more diverse and inclusive workplace by creating a system and space of support and familiarity for people groups that are in the minority in a specific workplace, environment, industry, or profession. All of the groups activities and engagements should align with the organizational purpose, vision, mission, values, and business practices.

These groups can be an integral component of your organizations commitment to help drive change in diversity, equity, and inclusion. It is also a great way to provide leadership and professional development opportunities for team members. Additionally, company ERGs and BRGs allows the organization to capitalize on the unique, valuable, and often overlooked resources, gifts, and talents of your employees. Research indicates that when ERGs or BRGs are established, employees become more engaged in exploring and identifying new & different ways to help benefit the organization. Thus, ERGs and BRGs not only help to showcase your organization's commitment to embracing diversity and fostering an inclusive culture, but they also contribute to business growth, employee engagement, and professional development.

ERGs and BRGs can help elevate the lives of its members in a way that benefits the entire organization through a series of education and empowerment initiatives.

Here are just a few ways that these types of groups have contributed to the education and development of organizations that I have worked with over the years…

> 1. Shared knowledge, raised cultural awareness, and act as a bridge across cultural issues

- improving the organizations cultural competence

2. Served as an much needed employee support system, provided numerous company-wide educational resources, facilitated professional growth opportunities, and encouraged new idea & information sharing with teams and leadership

3. Helped with recruitment and retention efforts

4. Supported new leadership strategies & ideas, as well as helped to improve managerial effectiveness and employee communications

5. Generate and deliver fresh, new, relevant, and innovative ideas for company processes, policies, and procedural changes

Mindful Communication

We discussed the importance of practicing mindfulness in chapter 5. We'll now spend some time defining and exploring the importance of mindful communication. Basically, Mindful Communication involves applying principles of mindfulness to the way that we correspond with others. This is a deliberate and thoughtful way of expressing oneself and listening to others. Mindful communication requires a high level of self awareness, patience, and the ability for you to control emotional reactions. By both adopting and promoting mindful communication, leaders can help ensure that everyone feels heard and understood.

Employing mindful communication also requires a willingness to meet people where they are. And that you don't project the same expectations that were placed on you, based on your situation, circumstance, or generation, onto others.

This is particularly true across the different generations. Keep in mind that every generation ushers in with it a New Era, with New Expressions, and New Expectations. And when you do find yourself dealing with an expectation gap, do your best to close that gap by working with your generational counterparts to help them elevate the experiences that they deliver, to better meet or simply manage the expectations, versus just lowering your expectations of them. When you choose to close the expectation gap by lowering your expectations of those that take a different approach than you, that can easily lead to you creating a false narrative, as it relates to the skill sets, abilities, or work ethic of that individual, and the people that share in their identity.

Encourage Perspective Taking: Leaders should encourage their teams to practice perspective taking – the act of viewing a situation from another person's viewpoint. This not only deepens understanding but it also helps to build and strengthen empathy. It helps people recognize and appreciate the experiences and feelings of others. This can easily be accomplished by leveraging the Heart, Head, & Hands Courageous Conversations model.

This simple three-phased model is explained further below.

You should always start with the **Heart,** by allowing and encouraging people to share how they feel about a specific topic. And don't stop at just exploring *"how"* someone feels, but also gain an understanding of *"why"* they feel that way. This is not about persuading people to agree with you, this is all about seeking understanding, and recognizing that you do not have to agree with someone to understand where they are coming from. Listening to someone else's story is one of the single most powerful ways to gain understanding. And once you've explored the heart phase, and have gained a deeper understanding of any obstacles to inclusion someone else may be facing, you are now in a much better position to contribute ideas that can help create a more inclusive solution. At that point, you are now ready to segue to the head phase.

As you enter into the **Head** phase of this engagement, this is where you begin to brainstorm ideas that can contribute to the greater good of all. The goal of the Head phase is to build out a strategic plan that helps to meet the specific needs of all stakeholders involved, based on the information shared in the heart phase and everyone's new level of understanding. During this phase, the conversations will need to be facilitated in a way that allows the participants to all collaborate on thoughts, ideas, and solutions as to how the members of the team or organization can create a healthier and stronger culture. This new and improved culture should reflect a culture of inclusion with policies, practices, and strong systems of engagement that rejects any and all elements of inequities, exclusion, or discrimination of any kind. This phase is as much about identifying a strategy as to how the collective can do better, as it is about each team member identifying how they can individually do better.

In the **Hands** phase, you put the plan into action and agree upon what work needs to be done to make a difference. This is the phase where you begin to apply the tactics that ladder up to the overarching strategy that was developed in the Head phase (phase 2). You should focus on developing SMART action steps that are in alignment with the overarching strategy, and then agree to do the work. Please note that SMART in this context refers to the acronym Specific - Measurable - Attainable - Relevant & Time bound.

This phase of the process should result in everyone on the team or in the organization, actively engaging each other. These engagements should be driven by a shared vision and purpose. This should all lead to a healthier culture of inclusion in which the organization, and the community that it serves, can all thrive, free of concerns of any form of exclusion, division, or inequities that may have been emanating from within the organization.

The ultimate purpose of the Heart, Head & Hands engagement is to equip and empower the members of your team, group, or organization with actionable insights, diverse perspectives, and relevant tools to break down any barriers and biases that may exist with people that are different from them. Additionally, the lessons learned throughout this process will help the participants to become more comfortable and equipped in getting to know people beyond stereotypes, preconceived notions, false narratives, and biases. It will also help them to recognize that what unites us is much greater than what we should be allowing to separate us.

Please note that each phase of the above process should be facilitated dialogue, and led by an experienced facilitator.

Here are some helpful tips, guidelines, and boundaries for facilitating courageous conversations

Courageous Conversations Guidelines & Boundaries:

1. Each participant will speak for themselves and their own experiences, and allow others to speak for themselves, with no pressure to represent an entire people group, or explain the actions of others.

2. No one will criticize the views of others or attempt to persuade others to think like they do.

3. Each participant will listen to understand and not to reply, even if you hear something from others that may be hard for you to hear.

4. Everyone will participate within the timelines that have been set forth by the facilitator and recognize the importance

of sharing talk-time with the other participants.

5. You will not interrupt anyone else when they're speaking, except to indicate that you cannot hear the speaker.

6. Everyone agrees to be an active participant, recognizing that they may be called upon to speak even when they have not raised their hand to speak, with the understanding that they can "pass" or "pass for now" on any question.

7. Everyone agrees to not judge others or make personal attacks on anyone even though you may not agree with what they say.

The goal here is to leverage the power of facilitated dialogue and empower the participants with the diverse perspectives and insights necessary to collaborate on ideas and solutions, to effect positive change for the greater good of all.

Leverage Technology: Language barriers are real, and can sometimes pose significant challenges when seeking to build bridges of understanding. However, advancements in technology, such as AI and other translation tools, can help bridge this gap, making communication more accessible and inclusive for everyone. New technologies have provided us all with amazing Bridge Building tools. Technology helps you to not only accelerate the process of Building Bridges, but it also helps to increase the efficacy and efficiency of the process. There are technology platforms that are designed to cater to organizations' specific diversity needs. Whether those needs be language driven, cultural, or geography based. New technologies are also available to help ensure that organizations can meet needs and accommodations of employees and team members of various backgrounds and abilities. Whether those needs be based on physical abilities, accessibilities, family needs, or other unforeseen circumstances.

Some ways that technology is being leveraged is to help remove biases from the hiring process. There are also digital platforms that exist that can help match potential candidates based on qualifications for the job, as well as specific accommodations that the employee may require. There are also numerous technology tools available that can help analyze individual employee needs. They help both the employee and the employer to adapt as needed, thus ensuring a seamless and effective employee integration. Whether it's software that adjusts its interface, based on a user's visual needs, or communication tools that cater to varied linguistic and auditory needs, there are technologies in place that help ensure everyone feels included.

And when it comes to Virtual Reality (VR) and Augmented Reality (AR), they aren't just for entertainment purposes anymore. They are both great technology tools for empathy training. Imagine, literally, stepping into someone else's shoes based on their day-to-day lived experiences. VR and AR have made this possible. These technologies are now being used to simulate experiences that allow employees to understand the challenges their colleagues might face. By walking a mile in their shoes, so to speak, employees can foster genuine empathy for their customers, colleagues and co-workers. According to a January 2024 article at inclusively.com (*14), a large multinational technology company utilized VR to simulate the experience of attending a meeting as a person that is hearing impaired, giving those who participated in the simulation a firsthand experience and understanding of the challenges of the hearing impaired. This prompted the participants to be more inclusive and empathetic in their interactions.

VR has also been utilized for bridge building purposes in the worlds of community impact and philanthropy. According to a June 2024 article posted by the National Peace Corps Association, VR has been described as an empathy generator (*15). Based on this article, studies have shown that, when done properly, Virtually Reality exercises can help increase empathy, compassion, and understanding in a way that other traditional media cannot. The article goes on to state that VR can offer a glimpse into lives and locales far from our own, fostering a sense of presence and shared experience. It's a tech tool that more nonprofits are starting to use, to give their supporters a new way to experience their mission.

I will say this though, when it comes to VR…as much as I am a fan of leveraging the power of technology and Artificial Intelligence (AI) to help advance our causes, and build stronger bridges of empathy and understanding, I don't believe that anything can, or should, replace the power and impact of real and direct human interaction and engagement whenever possible.

Challenge Stereotypes

Stereotypes can cloud our judgment and hamper understanding. Leaders should encourage their teams to recognize and challenge their stereotypes and assumptions about others. Hosting regular discussions, trainings, and immersive exercises can help to achieve this.

Stereotypes are formed based on your lived experiences. It's a result of assigning actions or behaviors of an individual of a specific identity or group to an entire people group of that same identity. Often times, the brain uses stereotypes as a way to help simplify the world for us by placing people, places, and things into easily clarified categories. The danger in this stereotypical thinking though, is it takes the simplification process too far, and we neglect to see people as individuals. No two people are exactly the same, even if they share the same race, gender, age, ethnicity, or even have the same parents. I know numerous sets of identical twins, who are still vastly different in their views, values, and behaviors.

There is an amazing TED Talk that does a phenomenal job of calling out the dangers of stereotyping. The TED Talk is called "The Danger of a Single Story" and is delivered by an incredibly brilliant woman named Chimamanda Ngozi Adichie. (*16). I encourage you to watch this TED Talk for yourself. By way of a quick overview, Adichie talks about how we, as people, create a single story about someone based on a single piece of information. That piece of information could simply be where that person is from. It could also be a person's financial status, social status, their sexual orientation, race, age, or any other singular piece of information we may know about them. And based on that one piece of information, we believe we know who they are, or what they are like.

For example, if someone is wealthy, you may think they don't know what it's like to struggle. If you see a young black person sitting in first class on a flight, you may assume they are an athlete or entertainer. Or if you see an elderly person working in a technology department of a store, you may assume they do not know anything about technology. These are all examples of the single stories that we form about people that are rooted in our own stereotypes. In her TED Talk, Adichie goes on to explain to us, that the actual danger of the single stories that we project, is not necessarily that the story or narrative that we have formed is incorrect. The danger is that it is incomplete.

None of us are one dimensional. Each of us are all multidimensional, multifaceted, dynamic beings, that cannot be defined by one singular attribute. Yes, someone may be wealthy, or an entertainer, or tech averse, but none of those attributes define all of who they are. Allow yourself the privilege of getting to know people beyond your single story of them. Allow yourself to go beyond the stereotype, and get to know them on a more human level.

Think about a time that you've been single-storied. A time when someone thought they knew all they needed to know about you, based on one piece of information; whether that information was your race, your size, your gender, your profession, or where you're from. Now take a minute to go through this simple exercise below and ask yourself the following questions…

1. How did it make you feel?
2. How did you respond?
3. Was it true?
4. Why do you think it happened?

Think about your responses to the above questions the next time you are in a situation where you may be about to single-story or stereotype someone. Hopefully, recalling how you felt when it happened to you will help you to avoid doing it to others.

The real danger of a single story isn't necessarily that it is inaccurate; although in many cases it is. The real danger of a single story is that it is always incomplete. Take time to get to know people for who they are, and not just what they look like, where they are from, or what they do for a living.

Chapter Summary

Overcoming obstacles and barriers to understanding is a process. It is a process that demands patience, commitment, and constant effort. By fostering a culture that prioritizes empathy, active listening, openness, education, mindful communication, perspective taking, and the use of technology, leaders can effectively surmount these obstacles and pave the way to build more empathetic and understanding workplaces and communities. On our collective journey towards building a more understanding society, every person matters, and every step counts.

Chapter 7: Building Bridges of Understanding

Understanding the Importance of Inclusivity

Inclusivity is not just about social justice or political correctness; it is about tapping into the richness of people's diverse perspectives and experiences. Different backgrounds bring unique perspectives and fresh ideas, enriching the decision making process, by revealing unseen pitfalls and uncovering new and innovative solutions. It prevents groupthink and the potential for overlooking significant risks or opportunities.

In the corporate world, decision making is often confined to upper management, executive leadership teams, or boards of directors. But this hierarchical approach can limit the scope of ideas. Similarly, in communities, decisions often lie in the hands of a select few influential individuals or institutions, creating an imbalance of power. This can easily lead to the marginalization of certain groups. To better promote inclusion, we must deconstruct these traditional decision-making structures and invite a broader spectrum of voices to the table.

I also recommend keeping these two things in mind…

1. The one's who are closest to an issue and feel the pain of that issue the most, are the one's best positioned to help identify the solution.

2. Wherever you have little-to-no inclusion, there will be little-to-no commitment. The more you include others in the solution to an issue, the more committed they will be to delivering on a solution for that issue.

The definition of understanding is to have complete comprehension, or to be sympathetically aware of someone else's feelings or way of thinking. To understand does not mean you have to agree. You can understand someone and still not agree. One of the most important steps to effective bridge building, is understanding. My experience has taught me that many disagreements and sources of discord and division, are rooted in people's selfish desires and a focus on what one party wants to get from the other party.

You want to get that person to agree with you, you want to get that person to admit that you're right, you want to get recognition, you want to get acknowledged, you want to get more money, status, or power. Many seeds of division are planted based on what you want to get. I would suggest to you that in order to be a better Bridge Builder; in all of your getting, that you get an understanding. That is one of the most powerful Bridge Building tools available to you. This is why it is so important to listen to understand and not just listen to reply. And that you seek first to understand before being understood.

Once you've extended the courtesy of seeking first to understand before being understood, the person that you are engaging with, will typically be more inclined to reciprocate, and extend you the same courtesy when it is your turn to be understood.

Implementing Inclusive Decision-Making
The first step in promoting inclusive decision-making, is acknowledging that there may be existing biases in your organization or community's decision-making processes. To help uncover what some of those biases may be, requires a deep-dive into the status quo, asking the hard

questions, and being ready to listen to uncomfortable truths. Asking questions like, how long has this process or policy been in place and is it outdated? Or, was this process or policy created with a specific people group in mind when it was created? The equity questions you should be asking yourself whenever you are developing new policies or procedures are as follows…

1. Will there be any impacts of inequity from this policy or procedure for any specific people group? If so, what are they?

2. Is there any specific people group that will benefit more, or is there any specific people group that will be burdened more once this decision is made? And if so, how?

3. What can the organization do to remove or mitigate any unintended consequences of any newly created policies or procedures?

Secondly, create an atmosphere of trust where everyone feels safe to voice their opinions without fear of retaliation or ridicule. Encourage open dialogue and provide channels for feedback from all stakeholders. This can be done through town hall meetings, suggestion boxes, online forums, or anonymous surveys.

Thirdly, make a conscious effort to involve underrepresented groups in decision making processes. It may require offering training, mentorship, or other additional resources to help ensure they can participate fully and effectively. This approach not only values diversity but also promotes equity, ensuring every member has the necessary tools to contribute.

Another aspect of inclusive decision making is transparency. All stakeholders should understand how the decisions are made, who makes them, and why. When people feel as though they are part of the process, and understand the rationale behind decisions, they are more likely to support the outcomes, even if those outcomes are different from their personal views. This makes it a lot easier for people to disagree and still commit. Remember, we should not always be seeking agreement, but we should always be seeking understanding.

Lastly, establish regular reviews of the decision-making processes to ensure they remain inclusive. This assessment can help to identify any unconscious biases or systemic barriers that may have crept in, while allowing for adjustments and improvements as you grow.

The Way Forward
Promoting an inclusive decision making process is not an overnight task; it is a long-term commitment that requires constant vigilance and conscious effort. It necessitates that organizational leaders possess a real and deep understanding of the words diversity, equity, inclusion, and empathy. A deep understanding of what each of these words truly mean, why they are important, and how they benefit the organization. Only then, can leaders ensure that major company-wide or community-wide decisions are shaped by a multitude of perspectives; thus leading to a more inclusive, a more productive, and a more harmonious environment for all.

Remember, as you build bridges of empathy and understanding, you must ensure those bridges are strong enough to carry everyone. Inclusion is not a destination but a journey, and this journey enriches you, your organizations, and your communities in countless ways. As you build these bridges, you should be asking yourself; how strong is my bridge? Is it a fragile straw bridge that will collapse at the first strong gust of wind? Is it a rickety wooden bridge that will give way to a storm? Or is it a strong reenforced steel bridge that can weather the storm and stand the test of time. Because the reality is… storms are going to come. Your organization and community will face challenges, and your bridges will be tested. And that's okay. That's what you want. Welcome the tests. Embrace the tests. That's how you know you are ready. Because whatever has been tested has been proven. Think about it… you wouldn't want to buy a car if you knew they hadn't tested the breaks. The same is true for the bridges you are building. You want to lead with the confidence of knowing that the bridges you are building will be able to weather the storms.

As the song writer says; "Sunny Days… everybody loves them. But can you stand the storm?" Or something like that. :-)

Chapter Summary
As we strive to build bridges of trust, empathy, and understanding, we must recognize the importance of inclusivity in the decision making processes within our organizations. We are in an era where the data consistently shows that embracing diversity, championing equity, and fostering inclusion, are cornerstones of successful corporations and thriving communities. To achieve success at the highest levels in this ever-evolving world that is growing more and more diverse everyday, the voices of all stakeholders must be sought, heard, and included. Not only does inclusivity foster a sense of belonging, but it also leads to more comprehensive, innovative, and effective decisions that stand the test of time.

Chapter 8: Empowering Leaders as Change Agents

Getting Started

To get started on building a culture of effective bridge builders, you must first equip your leaders with the necessary tools, information, and resources they need to serve as change agents. Your leaders play a pivotal role in shaping the culture, the values, and the behaviors of the organizations and communities they serve. And yes, the primary role of a leader is to serve. By equipping leaders with the tools, knowledge, and proper mindset, we can create a positive ripple effect that inspires empathy, fosters understanding, and drives meaningful change. In this chapter, we will explore proven strategies to empower leaders as change agents, enabling them to spearhead transformation, lead with empathy, and build a culture of trust.

Before we go any further on this topic, I want to revisit the definition of leadership from chapter 5…

Leadership is the *process* of influencing *people* by *providing* them with *purpose*, vision, and direction to accomplish the greater good of the team or organization.

If you recall, I highlighted the 4 P's of Leadership Principles earlier. I've revisited those principles below so that you don't have to flip back to chapter 5.

> **1. Process** - This lets us know that leadership is a process. It is what we do. It is a verb, not a noun. Leadership is reflected in our behavior and how we show up, not in out titles or status.
>
> **2. People** - This is who we do it for. Leadership should be

about the people. Many people in leadership positions based on their title, lose sight of this. The focus is too often placed on the bottom lines or profit margins. The bottom line and profits are obviously important to any business. But you do not get there without people. Leadership should be viewed as a role of responsibility that we have to the people that we've been given stewardship over, not a position of authority by which we should lord over them.

3. Providing - Leadership is about provision. This is how we do it. How are we providing for our people to ensure we are developing them in a way that helps them to reach their full potential? Leaders should make the time to get to know their people to ensure they are meeting them where they are and ensuring they are giving each individual what they need to succeed.

4. Purpose - This principle, as they say, is last but definitely not least. I would suggest that this is actually the foundational principle from which every leader should be building. This requires that you, as the leader, have a clear understanding of why you are there. What is your reason for being? What is your purpose beyond profit? And once you have gained that clarity of purpose, you should be able to clearly articulate that purpose to your team, and help them understand how their unique purpose ladders up to the overarching purpose of the organization. My favorite quote about purpose came from the late, great Myles Munroe. Mr.

Munroe taught us that; "when we don't know the purpose of something, abuse is inevitable".

Here is a more succinct breakdown of the 4 P's of Leadership and what they each represent…

1. Process = What we do
2. People = Who we do it for
3. Provision = How we do it
4. Purpose = Why we do it

It has been my experience that by applying these principles of what I refer to as *Inclusive Leadership*, you will experience transformational outcomes. I have experienced first-hand, and have seen the application of these principles result in leaders becoming the change agents that they aspire to be, and the change agents that the people need them to be.

Inclusive Leadership is defined as a commitment to meet people where they are, ensuring that they feel a strong sense of belonging and value, while providing them with the support they need to maximize their full potential.

Inclusive Leadership is not always easy, but it is extremely impactful and beneficial for the organization and everyone involved. Remember this little nugget about the power of inclusion that was shared in the previous chapter… *that where there is little-to-no inclusion, there will be little-to-no commitment.* One of the most powerful tools you can equip your leaders with, to help them serve as change agents, is to make sure they understand the power of inclusion. The more leaders include teams in the process to identifying and accomplishing organizational goals, the more committed their teams will be to helping them achieve the desired outcomes.

Cultivating Self-Awareness
The most effective change agents have a high level of self-awareness. In order for leaders to be the best change agents that they can be, they must first take a long, hard look at themselves. They must examine their own biases, assumptions, and privileges, to understand how those dynamics influence their leadership. How do these factors influence your leadership style, your perspectives, and your decisions?

This level of introspection allows leaders to approach situations with humility and openness. Encourage your leaders to engage in reflective practices, such as journaling, self-reflection, or seeking feedback from diverse perspectives. This will help to continuously grow their level of self-awareness.

Here is a simple 3-step approach that I take to building my own self-awareness and addressing and overcoming my own unconscious bias…

      1. Visualization
      2. Exploration
      3. Normalization

Visualization, involves visualizing someone of a completely different identity than you expected to see in certain positions, communities, or organizations. Our Unconscious Bias is typically triggered when we see someone different from who we expected to see in certain settings or situations, based on who and what we have become accustomed to seeing in these specific settings, situations, and environments. And when this occurs, we often behave or act differently towards people without even realizing it, hence the unconscious part of unconscious bias. The two biggest things to note about unconscious bias are...

> 1. It exists at a subconscious level, so there is a lack of awareness.
>
> 2. It is in complete opposition to the type of person we want to believe we are. So there is a degree of denial. Because none of us wants to think we view or treat others differently based on their identity.

I think it is critically important that everyone understands that having Unconscious Bias is by no means, any form of judgement or indictment on anyone. We all have some level of Unconscious Bias. It's simply a belief we have about a person or people group, usually rooted in stereotype, based on how we have been conditioned to think about them. This conditioning comes from a number of different things in our upbringing. Some factors include geography, education, parenting styles, media consumption, and numerous other trusted information sources in our lives.

After Visualization, the next step is **Examination**. Self-Examination to be more specific. This step involves examining your own actions and behaviors towards others after you've interacted with someone that has a different identity than you. The key to this step of the process is a willingness to be honest with yourself. Ask yourself did you behave differently towards the person, and if so, why? Why do you think you behaved differently? Once you've answered those questions (honestly), then be intentional about course-correcting any behavioral difference you identified the next time you engage with that person or someone that looks like them.

The third step to this 3-step process is **Normalization**. I personally think this step offers the greatest value when it comes to addressing our Unconscious Bias. Mostly because it minimizes how often any of the behaviors that are associated with Unconscious Bias are triggered. This step involves us normalizing diversity in our lives. In every aspect of our lives, both personally and professionally. By normalizing the degree of diversity in your life, it does not catch you 'off-guard' when you see a Woman, a Baby Boomer, a Black Person, a White person, a Gay person or any one of a different ethnicity than you. It doesn't 'throw you off' or confuse you to see someone in a certain position, role, situation, or environment, where you were expecting to see someone else. When you normalize diversity in your life, everyone belongs everywhere to you, regardless of their identity.

Enhancing Cultural Competence
Cultural Competence is the ability to understand, respect, and interact with people that have languages, values, beliefs, customs, and even abilities that differ from yours. And to do it in a way that appropriately acknowledges, considers, and then responds to those differences in the planning, the development, and the implementation of organizational policies, practices, programs, and procedures. Building bridges of trust, empathy, and understanding requires leaders to be deliberate and intentional about developing cultural competence. This requires you to proactively seek knowledge and understanding about different cultures, customs, languages, and even the communication styles of the people within your organization or community.

As we reflect back on the 4 P's of Inclusive Leadership, we can see how they apply when it comes to developing cultural competence...

Leadership is about *what* you do (process) - proactively seeking knowledge and understanding of different cultures,

Leadership is about *who* you do it for (people) - being inclusive of the culturally diverse people under your stewardship and to whom you have a responsibility

Leadership is about *how* you do it (provision) - providing culturally and linguistically relevant programming, materials, and procedures with everyone in mind

Leadership is about *why* you do it (purpose) - to ensure everyone has what they need to succeed and to help contribute to the greater good of the organization or community

Encourage leaders to engage in cross-cultural trainings, professional development workshops, or mentor opportunities that exposes them to diverse perspectives. Your leaders should actively seek opportunities to learn from people with different backgrounds and experiences than them, fostering a culture of inclusion within their team, organization or community.

Facilitating Dialogue
It is important for leaders to create safe spaces for open dialogue and collaboration, where diverse voices are encouraged and valued. When you create these safe spaces, it sends the message to your teams that you prioritize their mental health and psychological safety. In order to get the most out of these facilitated dialogues, be sure to encourage and empower individuals to share their experiences and perspectives freely. This can be achieved through

practices such as regular town hall meetings, employee resource groups, community conversations, or diversity and inclusion councils. Leaders should actively listen to the diverse viewpoints that are shared and lean into topics that address sensitive issues with empathy, grace, and respect.

Facilitating healthy and constructive dialogue is heavily reliant upon the right facilitator. The person that you choose to facilitate (or moderate) the dialogue must be someone whose only agenda is that of the greater good of the team, group, or participants. It cannot be someone with a white agenda, black agenda, blue agenda, left agenda, right agenda, or any agenda that favors any one specific individual, group, or cause.

The facilitator also needs to be someone that is both inspirational and aspirational. This person should be some that inspires others to be the best versions of themselves, and also someone that others view as informed and accomplished. This will lend to their credibility in the eyes of others. It is important that they see this person as someone they view to be qualified to lead the discussion.

Something else the facilitator needs to be mindful of, is that the purpose of the gathering and the dialogue is not about you. It is about how you, as the facilitator, are able to serve the people that are in attendance by being the best bridge builder you can possibly be. The facilitator's primary goals should be to create a safe space and evoke courageous conversation in a way that allows for the participants to hear, share, and learn from each other. To learn from each other's diverse perspectives, world views, and lived experiences. This should not be a forum to try and persuade other people to agree with you (the facilitator) or any of the other attendees. But instead, it should encourage, empower, and inspire others to share their stories with one another. I truly believe that story-telling is one of the single most powerful and influential ways to influence behavioral change. This is also the best way to help strengthen empathy. Because without hearing or knowing someone else's story to help you understand why they think or feel the way that they do, it is virtually impossible for you to empathize with them.

After each discussion, participants should all walk away with very clear and SMART (Specific, Measurable, Relevant & Time-Bound) Action Steps that can be applied right away. All done in an effort to help them become more effective change agents and better bridge builders themselves.

Building Partnerships

Change agents understand the power of collaboration. Encourage your leaders to build partnerships with external organizations, local community leaders, and other stakeholders. This will help broaden their impact. Forging these types of strategic alliances helps leaders to leverage collective resources, knowledge, and expertise to drive meaningful change. Collaborative initiatives, such as joint business ventures or community service projects, can foster relationships built on trust and shared goals that benefits the greater good of all the stakeholders and its members.

Empowering Others

Successful change agents empower others to become change agents themselves. Your leaders should prioritize professional development and mentorship of emerging leaders within their organizations and their communities. By providing pathways and opportunities for growth, and fostering an inclusive culture, leaders can create a ripple effect of community impact, empathy, and understanding, that extends well beyond their own circle of influence. And this should always be the goal as a leader; empowering others. And one of the best ways for you to empower others is giving the power that you've been given as a leader, back to the people that you've been called to lead. This is most effective when the power distribution is done according to each individuals unique gifts, talents, and passions.

Chapter Summary

Empowering leaders as change agents is another critical step in building bridges of trust, empathy, and understanding. By cultivating self-awareness, empathy, cultural competence, facilitating dialogue, building partnerships, and ultimately empowering others; leaders are able to ignite a powerful and long lasting transformation in their organizations and communities. When you take the time, as a leader, to empower others in a way that aligns with their gifts and passions, you teach them and inspire them to do the same for others. As the saying goes… you can teach what you know, but you reproduce who you are. If you want a team full of game changers and change agents, then empower them to be just that, by always leading by example. In other words, be the change you want to see in the world. Or in the case, be the change you want to see in the company.

Chapter 9: My Unforgettable 2020 Bridge Building Experience in Minneapolis

As I begin to bring a close to our time together with this book, I would be remiss if I did not share one final story about my own bridge building journey. During my time with the National Basketball Association (NBA), serving as the Chief Diversity & Inclusion Officer and eventually the Chief Impact Officer for my beloved Minnesota Timberwolves & Lynx, I lived through, and benefited from every single lesson shared throughout this book.

I started off consulting with the Timberwolves shortly after the tragic murder of George Floyd, and started with the organization on a full time basis in November of 2020. At that time, the City of Minneapolis was still suffering from all the social, racial, and political unrest from the murder of George Floyd. The city was literally and figuratively on fire. Then there was the added trauma, confusion, and uncertainties of the pandemic. This was an incredibly challenging time to be living in the city of Minneapolis, and to be there as a Bridge Builder brought its own set of additional challenges. People were hurt, and most weren't trying to hear the "can't we all just get along" speech. As a matter of fact, many people didn't want to "hear" anything at all. There was a strong sentiment that the time for talk had passed, it was now time for action! And I completely understood. But I also understood the importance and the value of facilitated dialogue with all the right stakeholders in order to take the appropriate action that the people were looking for.

The more people I spoke to, the more I learned just how much hurt, pain, and damage the city and its people had suffered. Particularly black people; and not just in the city of Minneapolis, but throughout the state of Minnesota. I learned that Minnesota was one of the worst states in the nation when it came to racial disparity and inequity, in five different categories. The categories include Education, Employment, Home Ownership, Health Care, and Poverty Rate. On the other hand, Minnesota is one of the wealthiest states in the nation and is ranked among the best states, in practically all the same categories where it has the worst racial disparities. This is known as the "Minnesota Paradox". (*17)

It soon became very clear to me why I was in Minneapolis, and the approach that I needed to take in order to stay in alignment with my assignment. I was not there solely for the Timberwolves & Lynx. I was there to play my part in helping to heal, reconcile, and resolve some of the damage that had been done, by serving as a community Bridge Builder. The Timberwolves & Lynx organization was the platform and distribution channel by which I was to deliver on that purpose.

I was also there to learn. It was abundantly clear to me that as much as I was there to teach, I was also there to learn. I was there to learn from the amazing Bridge Builders that were already based in Minneapolis doing the work, and had been doing so for years. Many of whom I've already mentioned earlier.

I was there to learn from Tony, Greg, James, Amelia, Kiera, Rod, Kathie, Martin, Meka, Anne, Chanda, Elizer, Leslie, Rebecca, Jen, Ethan, and several other corporate, non-profit, and community leaders. I'm a big believer that those of us who have been called to teach, must also be perpetual learners. So, in order for me to deliver on my assignment, and be the most impactful Bridge Builder I could be, I needed to learn as much as I could about the city, the culture, the challenges, and the opportunities that existed in my new city. I needed to stay true to the purpose of a bridge, in that it is built for the benefit of others. I needed to build and strengthen my cultural competence as it related to the state of Minnesota and the city of Minneapolis.

My assignment in Minneapolis was to do my part to help Build Bridges of trust, empathy, understanding, and love, at a time when the city needed it most.

One part of this story that I haven't shared with many people is that when I first received the job offer from the Timberwolves, I declined. Not because it wasn't an amazing opportunity. But because I didn't think I needed it. As a Speaker and Consultant, living in North Carolina, working for myself, and doing what I love; life was good. And although I was grateful, and humbled by the offer, I declined, because in my mind, I didn't need it.

About two weeks after I declined, I received another call from the team, asking me to reconsider. I remember that call like it was yesterday. I was with Chief Godwin, in his big ole Dodge Ram 3500 Pickup Truck. We were on our way back from a speaking engagement where we had just co-presented to a North Carolina Law Enforcement agency. He had overheard my portion of the conversation, and I filled him in on the rest after the call ended.

I remember him saying to me, that as much as he would hate to see me go, and leave behind all the great work that he and I were doing together, he thought the opportunity to work with the Timberwolves was an opportunity of a lifetime, and that

I should really consider it. After all, offers to work in the NBA don't come around everyday.

When I got home that day, I shared the news with my wife, and I asked her what she thought I should do. She said that I should pray about it. And just for the record, I did not pray about it the first time. That was more of a case of me leaning on my own understanding at that point, and in no ways acknowledging *Him.*

So what did I do? I prayed about it. I had learned over the course of my marriage (which was at 18 years married at the time), that my wife is usually right.

The response that I received after praying about it was powerful. God said to me, as clearly as I am typing these words, *'Tru, you declined the initial offer because you didn't think you needed what they had to offer. You were looking at it purely through a financial and material lens. But I'm not sending you there just for what you can get, I'm sending you there for what I want you to give. And you will get way more than you could ever possibly give in the process'.*

That conversation blew my mind. I was convicted in a way that I had never been before.

Needless to say, I gladly accepted the offer and officially made the move to Minneapolis in November of 2020.

Although I had officially answered the call to serve as a Bridge Builder in August of 2014, I probably learned more lessons about being a Bridge Builder in the 3 1/2 year timeframe between November 2020 and June 2024 than I did during the entire six years leading up to that season in my entire life.

Those lessons and insights started with Greg Cunningham and James Burroughs. Those two brothers supported me in ways that I didn't even know I needed. Even as a Bridge Builder myself, they helped to remind me of the importance of support. Just like every bridge needs support to stand and to be effective, so does every Bridge Builder. They helped crystallize the purpose of bridge building, in that it is not for the builder, it's for others.

You build bridges to provide access and elevation for others; which is what those two incredible leaders did for me. They both empowered me with the insights, information, support, and tools that I needed to be the change agent that I was called to be. And they did it without any hidden agenda, requests, or expectations from me, other than for me to do my part to help impact the community. Because they knew that by empowering me to serve as a Bride Builder and community change agent, based on the gifts and passions that I was given, it would contribute to the greater good of the entire community.

James and Greg were phenomenal resources for me into the corporate and philanthropic communities across Minnesota. They connected me freely and without reservation. And with every new person I met, I sought first to understand, before being understood. I wanted to learn about each individuals purpose, their mission, their goals, and their objectives. I wanted to understand their challenges, their pain points, and their contributions to healing, resolution, and reconciliation. I wanted to know these things so that I could understand where and how I could help. I wanted to understand how I could best leverage my gifts to add value to whatever they were already doing.

I knew my gifts, I trusted my gifts, and I was eager to share my gifts in ways that could help build whatever bridges needed to be built, for and with, whomever I had the benefit of being connected.

I realized, however, that their was a missing piece to the puzzle. There were bridges that I felt compelled to help build that I was not in position to build. Those were the community bridges. I'm talking about members of our community that many of the corporate, government, and even philanthropic agencies do a lot *for*, but don't often do a lot *with*.

I had the corporate relationships, the non-profit relationships, the Law Enforcement relationships, several connections in Education, and even a few government relationships. But I wasn't connected to the heart of the community. I wanted and I *needed* to be connected to the people in our community that were experiencing the inequities of those data points of racial disparity from the great 'Minnesota Paradox' that I discussed earlier. I needed and wanted to be connected to those that were being marginalized and discriminated against; those that were, and are, the most vulnerable members of our community.

Then, as fate would have it, along came my (now) good friends, Leslie E. Redmond and Rebecca Rabb. I met them on separate occasions, completely independent of each other.

Leslie was the former President of the Minneapolis Chapter of the NAACP, and we immediately hit it off. One of those people that you meet and it's just automatic! Leslie is an incredibly talented, committed, and compassionate activist and community leader. She was very gracious and extremely helpful in connecting me with key community stakeholders. And the community bridges were underway.

Rebecca worked for the Minnesota State Government in the Office of Justice Programs, also known as OJP. Rebecca was easily one of the most connected, no-nonsense, and remarkably gifted people I had met in the social justice space. Also very loyal, passionate, and protective when it came to community. She knew things that nobody else knew. And to this day, I still don't know how she stayed so informed about everything and everyone in the city of Minneapolis.

In her role at OJP, Rebecca focused on providing resources and support for families that have been victims of gun violence and other violent crimes. Rebecca was truly helping the people in our community who needed it most, and she knew all the other community leaders who were operating in a similar space.

After meeting Leslie and Rebecca, it was on and cracking from there!

Well, it wasn't quite on and cracking right out the gate with Rebecca, but we were able to get the bridge building efforts going not too long after our initial meeting.

Rebecca didn't initially like me or trust me when we first met, because of what I represented. In Rebecca's mind, I was just another corporate suit, that wanted more *from* the community than I wanted *for* the community. She believed that my only agenda for getting connected to the community was to see what I could take, versus what I wanted to contribute.

But after sharing my purpose, my vision, and my heart for community, she decided to give me a shot, and began taking me around to different communities, and introducing me to different grassroots community groups and leaders. The people, who much like her, were out there doing the work! And after I proved myself to be true (no pun intended), *then* it was on and cracking!

This was the missing piece for me. Because as I mentioned earlier, I was already connected with several corporate, non-profit, government, and education leaders. But I knew I needed to connect with community in a real way, to fully understand the complete landscape of difference. If I truly wanted to understand the complete landscape, I needed to understand it from those that were feeling the greatest sting of the Minnesota Paradox.

Leslie and Rebecca did this for me. They connected me with people like Lisa, Trae, Farji, Mickey, Lewiee, Tommy, and so many more grassroots community leaders who were serving the people who needed it most. All of whom have helped me gain a deeper understanding and greater appreciation for the true power of inclusion. Believe me when I tell you… those who are on the receiving end of the disparity and inequity, are the ones who are best positioned to determine what the solutions should be. I stand by that!

As much as the leaders in corporate and philanthropic spaces want to help transform and elevate the lives of those in need; until we are able to immerse ourselves into the world of those who we seek to serve, we will continue to be challenged to identify the best solutions. True empathy is built through hearing someone's story and through having shared experiences. The data is important, but it's not always enough. The transformational change that we seek is much more emotional than it is intellectual. And to truly and deeply understand how and why someone thinks or feels the way that they do, that requires empathy. It quickly became crystal clear to me, the importance of me doing my part to help connect corporate, non-profit and community. In order to do that, it required me to be intentional and deliberate about building and cultivating empathy and under-standing with the leadership among all the stakeholders.

My Minneapolis Bridge Building journey started at a time when the city was at its worst. I would often receive phone calls, emails and text messages from family and friends asking me why I was there. Because they knew I didn't have to be, and in their minds, if being in sports was never my dream, it didn't make sense to make such a sacrifice. My answer was always the same… "I am here because this is where I'm needed. And this is where I've been called to be". The part that I didn't always add, is I was there out of obedience. Out of obedience to the call that was placed on my life for that particular season of my life. I was there on assignment. And I am so glad that I said yes. The lessons that I've learned, the benefits that me and my family have received, and the fruit that was born out of that experience is far too abundant to truly quantify. I will share just a few of the outcomes from my time with the Timberwolves & Lynx that others have found ways to quantify.

Upon my arrival in November 2020, the organization was navigating through a lot of challenges. Some would say that they were not in a good place. This was obviously true for a lot of Minneapolis businesses and organizations on the heels of all of the unrest, damage, and trauma following the George Floyd murder.

But the bridge building work that began in November 2020, began to have more tangible results in 2022. In just two short years, the seeds of empathy, trust, love, hope, and understanding that we were planting and feeding, began to sprout. And these seeds were being planted everywhere, both internally and externally.

We were planting seeds of empathy & understanding among employees, fans, suppliers, corporate partners, community members, non-profits, government agencies, and everywhere in between. One thing that I kept in mind throughout this process was anything that can grow needs to be fed. I think we intuitively understand this from an agricultural and a biological standpoint. It's easy to understand how this applies to fruits, vegetables, plants, flowers, trees, and even people. But the principle of "whatever we feed will grow" is also as true for empathy, understanding, love, trust, and hope, as it is for hopelessness, fear, confusion, contempt, and hate. We chose to feed the former. And as those seeds began to bud and grow, they became the foundation for the bridges we needed to build.

And how, exactly did this impact the Timberwolves & Lynx organization you may ask? How did it impact me personally? What were some of the benefits and outcomes for buying into the belief that We Can All Be Bridge Builders? I'm glad you asked.

Here are just a few ways that others have quantified that impact in the two short years following the start of this 2020 Bridge Building journey...

1. 2022 – Named as one of Twin City Business (TCB) 100 People to Know for 2022

2. 2022 – Named as a Top DEI Leaders in the state of Minnesota by Minnesota Monthly

3. 2022 – Named as one of LinkedIn's Top 20 Voices in Sports

4. 2023 – Tru Pettigrew and the Timberwolves CEO, Ethan Casson, recognized among Sports Business Journal's (SBJ) ALL IN Leaders in Diversity, Equity, and Inclusion in Sports

5. 2023 – Recognized as one of the Twin Cities 200 Black Leaders you should know by the Minneapolis/St. Paul Business Journal

6. 2023 – Named as one of *The Minnesota 500*, a list of the most Powerful and Influential Leaders in Minnesota by Greenspring Media

7. 2023 – Selected to serve as one of the featured Speakers for TEDx Minneapolis

8. 2024 – Listed in the Minnesota African American Heritage Calendar for 2024 as an "African American Leader in Minnesota who has left and indelible mark on the landscape of our culture, state, and nation"

9. 2023 - 2024 Season – Minnesota Timberwolves recognized as the NBA's Leadership Inclusion Award Winner

10. 2023 - 2024 Season - PBWA (The Professional Writers Basketball Association) recognized Minnesota Timberwolves as the Brian McIntyre Media Relations Award recipient.

11. 2023 - 2024 Season - Minnesota Timberwolves were recognized as a finalist for Sports Team of The Year by Sports Business Journal (SBJ)

12. 2023 2024 Season - Minnesota Timberwolves player, Mike Conley, wins Teammate of The Year Award

13. 2023 - 2024 Season - Minnesota Timberwolves player, Naz Reid, wins Sixth Man of The Year Award

14. 2023 - 2024 Season - Minnesota Timberwolves player, Rudy Gobert, wins Defensive Player of the Year Award

15. 2023 - 2024 - Timberwolves player, Karl-Anthony Towns, wins the Kareem Abdul Jabbar Social Justice Champion Award

16. 2023 - 2024 Season - Minnesota Timberwolves advance to the NBA Western Conference Finals for the first time in 20 years

Even as I write this, I feel a strong sense of pride. I am extremely proud of every single member of the organization and the community that did the work and contributed to the above list. This is quite a list of accomplishments for a team that just 2 years prior was perceived by many as one of the most challenged organizations in the NBA, in one of the most challenged communities in the country. And by no means is that a knock on any of the talented members of the leadership team prior to 2020. Many of which I had the pleasure of working alongside and learning from. This includes the teams incredibly gifted and talented CEO, Ethan Casson. One of the best leaders that I've ever had the opportunity to work with.

Nor by any means, am I suggesting that any of the above accolades, recognitions, and accomplishments were achieved because of me. What I am saying is, I believe there is a correlation to all of these things happening because of an adopted culture of Bridge Building within the organization and community. I also think it's connected to the culture that was created by the people who all recognized that We Can All Be Bridge Builders. To me, this is one of those cases of correlation versus causation.

It has been my experience, that when members of an organization or community identify the purpose and importance of Building Bridges, and understand that they all have a part to play in Building those Bridges, then relevant outcomes like the ones listed above are possible.

When it comes to the roles that we all play as Bridge Builders, the best analogy I can offer is that of a highly functioning and performing human body. In that, we're all different body parts of the same body. We all have very different roles and functions, to help ensure the body performs at an optimum level. And when one part of the body is in pain or suffering, it affects the performance of the entire body. So let's make sure we are all doing our part to address the needs, health, and well being of all of our members.

Chapter 10: Lessons, Take-Aways, and Call-to-Action

Let us now take a moment to reflect on the various insights and lessons discussed throughout this book. Hopefully, our shared time together and exploration into the intricacies of leadership, diversity, inclusion, empathy, and understanding, has equipped you with practical bridge building tools, strategies and methodologies.

The primary challenges that we've addressed here, all revolve around differences and divisions among your corporate and community team members. We discussed that acknowledging these differences is our first step towards unity and meaningful connectivity.

From differences in experiences, culture, perspectives, to ways of problem-solving, each difference, whether nuanced or pronounced, adds to the richness and potential of a team. And that all starts with a willingness to engage in courageous conversations to help overcome barriers to understanding.

We delved into the importance of active listening, as a means to help us better understand, acknowledge, appreciate, and validate diverse viewpoints. By cultivating a culture of empathy and understanding, we encourage more open and honest dialogues, and a more collaborative environment.

Another crucial aspect we examined was the power of education and training. By promoting awareness, and facilitating inclusion workshops, we empower individuals to break stereotypes, reduce prejudices, and embrace diversity. Remember, the solution to ignorance should always be education.

We also underscored the essential role of leading by example. As a leader, your actions influence the behaviors and attitudes of your teams. By demonstrating inclusive behavior, we inspire others to do the same. As we learned from our friend Julius Campbell in "Remember The Titans" in his now classic one-liner response to Gerry Bertier; "attitude reflects leadership, captain!"

Lastly, we took a deep dive into the practice of conflict resolution and the transformation of differences into synergy. It's through our ability and our willingness to recognize our differences as strengths, rather than barriers, that we can truly unify our teams and communities.

The journey to building bridges across differences and divisions may be complex and challenging, but it is also deeply rewarding and essential for our progress. I believe it to be essential for the success and progress of our corporations, organizations, communities, and society as a whole. It requires grace, patience, understanding, and persistence, but most importantly, it demands a commitment to see and appreciate the value in every single individual we encounter.

As we close, it is my hope that this book has served as a guiding light on your journey towards fostering unity and harmony in leading your diverse teams and communities. The bridges we build today pave the way for a more inclusive, vibrant, and productive tomorrow.

Let's move forward with the understanding that our differences should not be sources of division, but our greatest strengths. Embrace them, celebrate them, and let them be the foundation of our unity.

In this ever-evolving world, it's not just about leading anymore; we need to lead inclusively and lead with purpose. I challenge you all to carry the torches of inclusive and purpose-driven leadership with the utmost level of pride. And in doing so, I believe that together, we will help create a brighter, more diverse, and harmonious future. A future that is not only hopeful, but a future filled with unlimited possibilities. A future where words like *Diversity*, *Equity*, and *Inclusion*, are not just words that we weaponize against each other, but a powerful reality that has been achieved and normalized in every realm of our society across the globe. Let's recognize that these words are not divisive. But based on the very definition of these words, they reflect, represent and inspire innovation, collaboration, fairness, progress, and belonging.

Diversity by definition is the state of being different. It is a state of being. It does not do anything. It simply exists. It is what it is. It will always exist. It's not something that we should seek to do away with. The reality is, we couldn't even if we wanted to. It is not related to race, age, gender, sexual orientation, or even people for that matter. It is the gift of diversity that allows us to have variety in life. It empowers us to be more innovative when it comes to new ideas, new services, new products, and new solutions. It is a gift. And that gift is available to us all.

The definition of equity is fair and impartial treatment. That is something we should all strive for. We begin teaching our kids about the importance of fairness from the time they can first walk. We've created an entire judicial system with judges, and entire sports industry with referees and umpires, and learning institutions with teachers and administrators, whose very roles exist to ensure and promote fairness.

I don't think anyone would ever suggest that fair and impartial treatment for others is a harmful or divisive practice.

Inclusion by definition is the actions and behaviors we display to create a sense of belonging for others. Who doesn't want to feel like they belong? If I'm not mistaken, this is one of the basic human needs on Maslow's Hierarchy of Needs. It is the third fundamental need listed right after basic physiological needs, and the need for safety and security. Love and belonging is right there! Again, it would be hard to suggest that we should not prioritize providing people with their basic human need of belonging. It is a need that we all have, and a need that we are all capable of providing for each other. And that need is even greater when we find ourselves in an environment where we are in the minority. There is nothing hurtful, harmful, or divisive about a person's basic human need for love and belonging.

It has been my understanding of these 3 words, and my willingness to apply them appropriately in my service to others, that has allowed me to make my greatest impact in life. And ultimately, that is how we measure the success of our service; the impact that we are able to make in and on the lives of others.

Impact is defined as having a strong effect or influence on someone, something, or a situation. We all do that in some shape or form everyday. There are three primary areas of impact that you can make, and those 3 areas are Social Impact, Cultural Impact, and Community Impact.

In what ways are you impacting the lives of others? Take a look at each form of impact and really give that some thought…

Social Impact - This is defined as any significant or positive change that solves or addresses any social injustice, inequities, or challenges

Cultural Impact - This is the shift and evolution in actions, decisions, and behaviors of a group based on an understanding of shared ideas, values, and beliefs of the collective group

Community Impact - This is the lasting systemic, systematic, or structural change that a group of people are able to make within a specific community

We all have the opportunity to make an impact in at least one of these areas everyday. And often times, in all of them. The question is… Are you willing to be intentional about making a positive social, cultural, or community impact?

Whether we're discussing Diversity, Equity, Inclusion, or Impact, none of these words or terms are harmful. In fact, they are all amazing bridge building tools.

It's the application of how the tool is used by the person using the tool that can be harmful. This is true for any tool. A hammer can be used as a tool by which you can build, or a weapon by which you can destroy and cause great harm. The choice is up to you. Will you use these tools to connect and build, or weapons to divide and destroy? I pray that you all choose the former.

Some of my biggest learnings from my journey has been understanding the most effective *Tools of a Bridge Builder,* the greatest *Attributes of a Bridge Builder*, and the biggest *Benefits of a Bridge Builder.*

Here are my breakdowns for each...

Tools of a Bridge Builder
In my experience, the most effective tools of a Bridge Builder are clarity of Purpose, Vision, and Mission.

Let's start with purpose. I believe clarity of purpose is paramount when you are building bridges across differences. The purpose of a bridge is to serve as a resource to connect people across vast territory, terrain, distances, or differences, that are otherwise impassable. Bridges exist to connect people from where they are, to where they desire to be. Once you understand that, you must also understand why the specific bridge you are building is necessary. What challenges, struggles, obstacles, or differences will people no longer struggle with once they have crossed your bridge?

Vision is the next important tool to have in your toolbox. While purpose is the reason for being, vision is seeing where you are going. And as the quote goes… "without a vision, the people will perish!" And I most definitely don't want any of you to perish. So, ask yourself, what is your vision for the bridge building work that you are doing? Where are you going with it? For me, my bridge building vision is to serve as the world's most valued and trusted resource when it comes to helping people understand how to connect across differences. That's the vision! It's very important that your vision is aspirational and serves as more of a journey than a destination. That way you are constantly striving to reach that peak, and you are in constant pursuit of excellence for yourself and others.

Your third best bridge building tool is mission. In the same way that you should view purpose as *being*, and vision as *seeing*; you should view mission as *doing*. The question you should ask yourself here, to ensure you are staying on mission, is; what are you *doing* to get to where you are *going*? Are you speaking, are you facilitating gatherings, are you writing books or articles, are you teaching classes, are you designing clothes, and the list goes on. How are you leveraging your gifts to achieve your vision and fulfill your purpose? For me, I am leveraging my gifts of speech, communication, and facilitation to empower others to co-create solutions that helps them and their organizations to overcome biases and build stronger cultures of inclusion. Once you've identified your purpose, vision, and mission, you will have all the tools you need to build the bridges you've been called to build.

Attributes of a Bridge Builder

In my experience, the three primary attributes of an effective bridge builder are Grace, Empathy, and Understanding. Grace, by definition, is the undeserving favor that we all receive. You did not do anything to earn it. As a matter of fact, it usually requires a high level of care and compassion from the person who is extending you grace, to overlook your offensive behavior or misdeed.

Grace is such an important attribute of a bridge builder, because you will inevitably be on the receiving end of someone else's offense. An offense that will not always be intentional or malicious. More often than not, the offenses that we experience are rooted in other people's ignorance. They simply lack the knowledge and understanding of why or how what they did or said was offensive. This is where grace comes in.

In those moments when you feel slighted or flat out offended by what someone else does or says; your willingness to show them grace, and extend unsolicited forgiveness… that is one of the strongest bridge building attributes you can embody. And there will be times when you feel like people don't deserve your grace. And I get it. I even agree. Just remember though… it wouldn't be grace if they deserved it.

The next primary attribute of a bridge builder is Empathy. Without empathy, I believe that it is virtually impossible to be an effective bridge builder. Empathy helps to place you in someone else's shoes and see things from their perspective. And in some cases, it helps you to better understand how they feel about an issue. But even more important than understanding *how* someone else sees, thinks, or feels about an issue; empathy helps you to understand *why* they see, think, or feel that way.

Once you understand *how* and *why* someone else feels the way they do about something, you realize that had you been in their shoes, and had the same lived experience as them, you just might see, think, or feel the same way as they do. And with that understanding, you are less inclined to take their reaction or response personally, just because it differs from yours. You are also in a much better position and headspace to help identify solutions, and even help resolve any issue that a differing of perspectives may have caused.

Understanding is the third attribute that I find extremely important for bridge builders. As you may recall from earlier in the book, I talked about the importance of listening to understand. I also talked about seeking first to understand before being understood. And in all your getting, to get an understanding. Hopefully those points help highlight the importance of the attribute of understanding. This attribute is also one that we probably have the most opportunity to put into practice.

When engaged in conversations where differences emerge, take the time to seek an understanding of what the other person is attempting to convey. Consider that there may actually be some validity to what they are saying. Bridge building is not about seeking agreement, it is about seeking understanding.

Benefits of a Bridge Builder
There are many benefits to being a bridge builder. And those benefits extend far beyond you. They impact those around you for whom the bridges have been built. And if the bridges are strong enough, they even extend far beyond the people that you are able to touch today, and they will impact generations of

people to come, that you will never even meet.

There is something really special about knowing, that the work that you are doing will impact future generations. I read somewhere, that one of the priorities for our societal leaders should be securing the blessings of liberty, for ourselves, and our posterity. (that's from the preamble to the US Constitution by the way).

I believe we all have a responsibility to build bridges for those that come after us. Much like our friend Will Allen Drumgoole, who wrote the poem "The Bridge Builder". If you've never read that poem, no worries. Just keep reading. But to give you a quick overview, the poem speaks about an old man who had made his way across an angry stream, and then took the time to build a bridge after he had already made it across. And when he was questioned about why he took the time, energy, effort, and risk, to build a bridge across a stream that he had already crossed, his reply was that he was building the bridge for the next passerby, who may not be as fortunate as him.

As I think about "The Bridge Builder" poem and the commitment to our posterity outlined in the preamble to the US Constitution, I am reminded that one of the biggest benefits of being a bridge builder is **Access**.

When you think about a bridge, one of its primary purposes is to provide you with access to places that you otherwise would not be able to reach. I believe that each generation bears the responsibility to build bridges that provide ease of access and connectivity for themselves and for the generations that follow.

*"The Bridge Builder" poem, by Will Allen Drumgoole (*18)* does a much better job expressing this sentiment of building bridges for the purposes of providing access for those that come after us. I've taken the liberty to share it with you on the following page…

"The Bridge Builder"

By Will Allen Drumgoole

An old man going a lone highway,
Came, at the evening cold and gray,
To a chasm vast and deep and wide,
Through which was flowing a sullen tide,
The old man crossed in the twilight dim,
The sullen stream had no fear for him;
But he turned when safe on the other side
And built a bridge to span the tide.

"Old man," said a fellow pilgrim near,
"You are wasting your strength with building here;
Your journey will end with the ending day,
You never again will pass this way;
You've crossed the chasm, deep and wide,
Why build this bridge at evening tide?"

The builder lifted his old gray head;
"Good friend, in the path I have come," he said,
"There follows after me today,
A youth whose feet must pass this way,
This stream that has been as naught to me
To that fair-haired youth may a pitfall be;
He, too, must cross in the twilight dim;
Good friend, I am building this bridge for him!"

The second biggest benefit of a bridge builder is the **Connection** that it provides. Again, this benefit is not limited or relegated to just you. Building Bridges, and the actual bridges that you build, help connect you to people, places, and things that you never even knew existed.

Bridges provide you with pathways and opportunities that will elevate your life to levels that you may have never even considered. When I first began building bridges between Law Enforcement and the Black Community back in 2014 in Cary, NC, I had no idea that those bridges would connect me with people, places, and things that would lead me to the NBA with the Minnesota Timberwolves & Lynx in the city of Minneapolis. And when I began building bridges with corporations, non-profits, and community groups in Minneapolis, I had no idea that it would connect me with people, places, and experiences that would eventually lead to this very book that you are reading right now. Simply put, when you become a bridge builder, it helps to create connections and opportunities that you never even knew existed.

And the third benefit of a being a bridge builder that I will share, is **Transformation**. Bridge Building work is transformational. It changes hearts and minds. And not just the hearts and minds of the people that you are building for, it changes your heart, and your mind, in ways and areas that you didn't even know you needed to be transformed.

I am a better husband, I am a better father, I am a better brother, friend, leader, and overall human, because of the bridge building work that I do. I am able to see the world through what I call heart vision. And what I mean by that is best captured in this quote by Doe Zantamata… "When I see you through my eyes, I think that we are different. But when I see you through my heart, I know we are the same". This is not to suggest that I am completely naive to the evildoers in the world and those that seek to do people harm based on their own issues of discrimination, isms, and malice. I have just grown to learn that they are in the minority in this world. And the vast majority of us want the same thing, and share the same values.

Bridge Building does not require an advanced degree. It doesn't require special gifts, wealth, or status. It does not require fame, or notoriety. Being a Bridge Builder is a heart condition. It's only requirements are that you have a heart of service, and the willingness to do the things that other people won't do. We all have the ability to do things that other people can't do.

My question and my challenge to you is this; are you willing to do the things that other people won't do? Things like being intentional about building your empathy muscles. Things like listening to understand instead of listening to reply. Seeking first to understand before seeking to be understood. Meeting people where they are instead of where you think they should be. Loving *people* where they are even when you don't love where they are. These are all choices.

It's easy to destroy people, places, and things. It takes a lot more effort and intentionality to build. I pray that you choose the latter.

This bridge building journey has helped to elevate my life in many ways. It taught me the importance of not conforming to ways of the rest of the world based on other peoples ignorance, but instead, to be transformed my the renewal of my own mind. I have learned that there is power in my words. I have learned that life and death is literally in the power of the tongue.

I have learned that what I allow in my heart, determines what comes out of my mouth and that out of the abundance of the heart the mouth speaks. I have learned that above all things, I should guard my heart, because it's the things of the heart that will dictate the course of my life. And because of that, I refuse to allow my heart to be filled with hate, fear, malice, contempt, apathy, or any form of discrimination. Because those are not the things that I want to dictate the course of my life.

I choose to fill my heart with love, courage, compassion, patience, empathy, and understanding. In other words, this bridge building journey has completely transformed my life. And I am now able to live in abundance in every dimension of my life.

There are tremendous benefits to being a bridge builder. But even if the only benefits were the three that I shared above *(Access, Connection & Transformation)*, that would be enough for me to commit to this work a thousand times over. It has provided me with a life of purpose, fulfillment, and abundance. And this type of purpose-filled, abundant life is not relegated to just a select few. We Can All Be Bridge Builders!

So, no matter how challenging or daunting the task before us may appear… Let's Keep Building!

Additional Resources to Becoming a Better Bridge Builder:

Please follow my "Tuesday's With Tru" Social Media posts. They are posted every Tuesday on LinkedIn, Instagram, Tik Tok, and Facebook. Follow these messages for weekly insights on how to Build Bridges of Trust, Legitimacy, Empathy, and Understanding in your organization or community.

By joining me on "Tuesday's With Tru" and by scheduling one of my signature Talks or Workshops, you will unlock a wealth of insights, thought-provoking discussions, and SMART action steps to Building Bridges of connectivity across any divide you and your team may be facing.

Together, we can make a difference! One Bridge at a time! To schedule one of my Signature Talks or Workshops, go to the website below to get started:

www.Tru-Access.com

Tru Access Signature Talks & Workshops

Are you passionate about fostering a world where empathy and understanding prevail? Are you interested in learning how you can leverage the power of Leadership, Inclusion, and Purpose to strengthen team engagement, enhance performance, improve productivity, and increase profitability? If so, then let's dive deeper into one of the below topics by arranging for one of my signature talks or workshops to help you do just that. You can learn more at www.Tru-Access.com. Some of my Signature Talks and Workshops are listed on the following pages…

We Can All Be Bridge Builders - We live in a world that is plagued with division in practically every facet of life; socially, politically, racially, and so much more. We need people to understand how to build bridges across those divides now more than ever. And most of us want to be the Bridge Builders that the world so desperately needs. You just don't know how. Most of you are tired of the pain, suffering, and destruction that these seemingly endless seeds of division are all causing in your life. And you want to know how to help reconcile, heal, and resolve these differences. This session serves as a roadmap for all who attend, to understand how to Build Bridges of Trust, Legitimacy, Empathy and Understanding across any and all differences.

DEI & WHY - During this session, participants walk away with clearly articulated definitions of Diversity, Equity & Inclusion. These definitions will serve as the foundation from which to build. Participants will then be engaged in dialogue that will help them better understand how these three components are linked, but also still very distinct. The main purpose and key take-a-way for this session is for defining and applying Diversity, Equity, and Inclusion in a way that provides attendees with a clear roadmap, as to why each of these components are important, how to apply them in a seamlessly integrated manner, and what the expected outcomes should be when done effectively.

Leading With Purpose - People are not only seeking purpose in their personal lives, but they want to align themselves with organizations that have, and provide them with a sense of purpose. People want to align themselves with brands and organizations who are "Leading With Purpose." Learn what it takes to become one of those people or organizations. This session equips leaders with tools to effectively Lead With Purpose, while simultaneously empowering your team members with *The 4 P's of Purpose-Driven Leadership Principles* and *The 5 C's of Purpose-Driven Leadership.*

Tapping into Your Greatness - Greatness is inside all of us. It is not some rare attribute that is reserved for a select few. It is a choice that is available to us all. This session helps to reveal the greatness inside of each participant. This is done through interactive, engaging, and fun exercises and story-telling. All attendees from this session walk away inspired; knowing that they have been created to achieve greatness in every dimension of their lives, and empowered with the tools and understanding of how to tap into that greatness. Key take-a-ways include a clear understanding of *why* they should tap into their greatness, a roadmap of *how* to tap into their greatness, and *what* the benefits are for themselves and those around them when they do.

Becoming More Conscious of Your Unconscious Bias - One of the first things to understand about Unconscious Bias, also known as Implicit Bias, is that it affects us all. Two of the biggest challenges with Unconscious Bias, is one…that it exists at a subconscious level and two… it is in exact opposition of who we'd like to believe we are. So there is an element of unawareness and an element of denial that we must contend with when it comes to overcoming our unconscious bias. In this session, attendees will clearly define unconscious bias, understand the importance of combatting unconscious bias, and develop tools to overcome unconscious bias.

Inclusive Leadership - We are at a point in our world's history where we are the most diverse we've ever been. And we are growing more and more diverse year over year. It has become paramount to understand how to lead across all of those forms of diversity through Inclusive Leadership. This session provides attendees with valuable inclusive leadership tips, tools, and strategies that they can effectively employ at every level of leadership. Benefits include a more inclusive culture where the people are inclined to co-create and collaborate on thoughts, ideas, and solutions that benefit the entire organization and the greater good of all involved.

Moving Beyond Diversity - Many organizations have invested tremendous amounts of resources in an attempt to increase diversity. And understandably so, evidence demonstrates that diversity helps drive innovation, improves creativity, allows for better recruiting, and less turnover. Even with that being the case, we are seeing more and more organizations walk away from their diversity efforts. One, of the many reasons that this may be occurring, is organizations are quickly realizing that diversity alone, cannot be the end-goal. Instead, the intentional act of developing more open and inclusive environments for team members and employees, is now the greatest need and challenge. In this session, attendees learn how to move beyond diversity, and satisfy the basic human craving of inclusive environments in which to live, work, and play.

Courageous Conversations on Race - This is a series of facilitated dialogue designed to help build bridges of trust and understanding across racial differences, and foster a healthier culture of inclusion for all to thrive. During this 3-part series, attendees engage in, and learn how to leverage the power of facilitated dialogue. These sessions guide the participants on a journey from the Heart to the Head to the Hands. We start with sharing our hearts to build empathy, then segue to the head to collaborate on ideas, and wrap up with SMART Action steps that allow us to put our hands to the plow and start doing the work.

Leading Across the Generations - Each New Generation ushers in a New Era, with New Expressions, and New Expectations. To thrive in this new era, organizations must be willing to adopt and employ a cross-generational leadership approach.

This session helps attendees understand how to be more effective 21st century leaders by leveraging the power of insight, influence, and generational inclusion. Attendees will walk away with a proven cross generational leadership model that can be applied right away!

Discovering Your Personal and Professional GPS to Purpose - This highly celebrated course has greatly impacted the lives of everyone who has participated. All who participate are guided to their unique purpose in life! We all come equipped with our own internal GPS. Our systems have already been pre-programmed to guide us to our purpose. The key to getting there is recognizing that it exists, and learning to listen to it. Your GPS is an acronym for your Gifts (G), your Passions (P) and your Service (S). After taking this course, you will have clarity of where and how to better focus your time, attention, and resources, on all the stressful and hectic demands that life sends your way.

Thank you for joining me on this Bridge Building journey. I truly hope you found the information helpful and that through the content of this book, I was able to add some value to your life, your business, your family, and your community.

I commend you for all the impact you have already made through your Bridge Building efforts. And Congratulations in advance for all the impact you will make moving forward.

Let's Keep Building!

Sources:

(*1) - https://www.ussc.edu.au/analysis/america-more-divided-than-at-any-time-since-civil-war

(*2) - https://en.wikipedia.org/wiki/Killing_of_Michael_Brown

(*3) - https://en.wikipedia.org/wiki/Murder_of_George_Floyd

(4*) - https://www.shrm.org/executive-network/insights/5-generations-now-working-together-heres-how-smart-leaders-making

(*5) - https://newsroom.wf.com/English/news-releases/news-release-details/2024/New-Report-Finds-Growth-of-Women-Business-Owners-Outpaces-the-Market/default.aspx#:~:text=From%202019%20to%202023%2C%20women,in%20revenue%20to%20the%20economy

(*6) - https://williamsinstitute.law.ucla.edu/publications/adult-lgbt-pop-us/

(*7) - https://www.cdc.gov/ncbddd/disabilityandhealth/features/disability-prevalence-rural-urban.html#:~:text=Approximately%20one%20in%20four%20adults,with%20at%20least%20one%20disability

(*8) - https://www.census.gov/newsroom/facts-for-features/2023/hispanic-heritage-month.html#:~:text=63.7%20million,19.1%25%20of%20the%20total%20population

(*9) - https://www.pewresearch.org/social-trends/2021/03/25/the-growing-diversity-of-black-america/

(*10) - https://www.pewresearch.org/short-reads/2021/04/29/key-facts-about-asian-americans/

(*11) - https://www.wuga.org/local-news/2019-03-28/minority-groups-in-u-s-have-combined-buying-power-of-3-9-trillion#:~:text=Minority%20-Groups%20in%20U.S.%20Have%20Combined%20Buying%20Power%20of%20%243.9%20Trillion,-WUGA%20%7C%20By%20Alexia&text=U.S.%20minorities%20are%20making%20financial,but%20not%20at%20equal%20rates

(*12) - https://www.mckinsey.com/capabilities/people-and-organizational-performance/our-insights/its-cool-to-be-kind-the-value-of-empathy-at-work

(*13) - https://medium.com/@davegray/updated-empathy-map-canvas-46df22df3c8a

(*14) - https://www.inclusively.com/role-of-tech-in-facilitating-dei/

(*15) - https://www.peacecorpsconnect.org/virtual-empathy/

(*16) - https://www.hhh.umn.edu/research-centers/roy-wilkins-center-human-relations-and-social-justice/minnesota-paradox

(*17) - https://www.ted.com/talks/chimamanda_ngozi_adichie_the_danger_of_a_single_story?language=en

(*18) - https://www.poetryfoundation.org/poems/52702/the-bridge-builder

Printed in the USA
CPSIA information can be obtained
at www.ICGtesting.com
LVHW021747120924
790643LV00013B/707